Where Top-down, Where-Bottom-up?

Silke Tönshoff/Andreas Weida (eds.)

Where Top-down, Where Bottom-up?

Selected Issues for Regional Strategies in the European Union

PETER LANG
Frankfurt am Main · Berlin · Bern · Bruxelles · New York · Oxford · Wien

Bibliographic Information published by the Deutsche Nationalbibliothek

The Deutsche Nationalbibliothek lists this publication in the Deutsche Nationalbibliografie; detailed bibliographic data is available in the internet at <http://www.d-nb.de>.

ISBN 978-3-631-57203-0

www.peterlang.de

Where top-down, where bottom-up?
Selected issues for regional strategies in the European Union

Preface

"We are doing it anyway" - The necessity for regional policy-makers to find a balance between shaping and adapting to structural change is well-known. But to what extent does this apply to a European strategy with a "soft" governance process relying largely on benchmarking and peer pressure - the Lisbon Strategy for Growth and Jobs?

Paradigms for an increase of competitiveness – also regional competitiveness - spelled out so often and vigorously lose their degree of assertiveness, when turning to economic theory for their foundations. Regional economics have held from the beginning a special place in overall economic theory. Tensions between different basic convictions, inherent in every economic concept, have been aggravated by the fact of different political decision levels.

A macro-economic understanding of regional competitiveness is often seen as imprecise if not simply defined as the outcome in terms of economic growth. Moreover, regional competitiveness cannot be translated as a derivative of national competitiveness. The analogy between an economy and a firm does not even hold for the Member State level and even less so when taking into account the transfer of substantial economic sovereignty to the European level. Further limitations stem from monetary policy and the specific set-up of the Stability and Growth Pact. Finally, the adjustment mechanisms of international trade, in particular exchange rate movements, do not exist at the sub-national level.

While in the beginning of the nineties it seemed tempting to do away with setting economically sound priorities and to regard modern regional planning from a firm perspective in a market environment, only recently competitiveness is seen with a broader perspective as including environmental and social factors for generating better living-standards. The sources and conditions of robust economic growth across EU 27 on the regional level vary largely. Nevertheless, bottom-up planning by regional policy makers can contribute to macro-economic growth. Both policy-makers and economic advisers also have to be explicit on the criteria of evaluating the success of regional economic concepts.

This book comprises Working Papers on selected issues by trained economists and political scientists from different EU Member States that have all gained practical experience in European Union institutions and whose academic interest has always included the regional factor. Some months before the mid-term review of the re-launched Lisbon Strategy (2005-2010) seems to be a worthwhile point in time for contributing to the debate.

The contributors are:
- Bernard Chane-Kune (Policy Analyst at the Committee of the Regions)
- Marjorie Jouen (Member of cabinet of the President of the Committee of the Regions; previously Head of Unit at the Department of Treasury and Trade, France and advisor on Regional Issues at Notre Europe)
- Dr. Silke Tönshoff (Policy Analyst at the Committee of the Regions; previously at RAND Corporation Berlin/Leiden)
- Dr. Andreas Weida (General Secretariat of the Council of the European Union; Directorate General C - Internal Market, previously Researcher at the University of Wuppertal, Germany)

Jouen is analyzing the options of endogenous local development and Foreign Direct Investment as development strategies. She describes the benefits and components as well as the intrinsic weaknesses and prospects of local endogenous development. In his first contribution Weida sheds some light on the incoherence of the Lisbon approach as having borrowed elements originating from sometimes irreconcilable economic theories. Though the re-launch of the Lisbon Strategy in 2005 has improved matters to some extent, the current focus on benchmarks and well-intended objectives cannot compensate for major deficiencies in the overall approach. The Lisbon Strategy has delivered a blueprint for the European economic development which is based for its governance structure largely on the partnership between the different stake-holders and actors on the various governance levels. Tönshoff is analyzing inhowfar this approach has been applied after the revision of the Lisbon Strategy in 2005. Chane-Kune describes to what extent the notion of decentralized cooperation has had an influence on current concepts of development policy. While some Member States have created significant funds for decentralized cooperation and the participation of regional and local is in principle undisputed, the European Union still does not have a homogenous approach in this issue. In his second contribution, Weida argues that the issue of tax harmonisation will return to the agenda of EU politics. Although a consensus on the importance of the criteria and objectives of tax policy will never be complete, a lack of workable cooperation will eventually have negative repercussions in all European member States independent of their economic policy approach.

Certainly, the opinions expressed in the contributions are exclusively those of the authors and are not in any way related to official positions, plans or intentions of the European Institutions.

The Editors Autumn 2007

Contents

Marjorie Jouen

Endogenous Local Development *versus* Foreign Direct Investment Strategies: Are there alternative regional options in EU 27?

Today, there are very few European regions which do not have economic development strategies and which claim to give themselves only to the good will and on the initiative of the companies to ensure their prosperity and their future.

This may be explained by the obligations to which the local authorities had to answer during the last thirty years. Their competences underwent a progressive extension of the social field towards the economic field, while the industrial restructurings became gradually regular in the life of the companies and the regions and that it appeared crucial to anticipate them. This development was strongly accompanied and encouraged by the European cohesion policy, conceived at the end of the 1980s like a "flanking" policy of the Single Market to reduce the regional disparities. More recently, the objective of convergence, mainly focused on the less-developed regions, was integrated in an EU-wide attempt to improve Europe's competitiveness at a global level.

Beyond the general guidelines common to the EU 27, if one takes account of the diversity of the local situations, of their potential and of the aspirations, the picture of cities and regions' current strategies to support the economy and jobs shows fortunately a wide variety of approaches, a broad range from race to attract external investments until local endogenous development associated with the social economy. This variety constitutes the wealth of Europe and probably one of its major assets.

However, looking back at the ground covered over more than 20 years, uniformity and standardization seems to have made progress: the difficulty of the "bottom-up" development of stating oneself as a genuine alternative development strategy in face of the development based on the foreign direct investments' attractiveness constitutes a good illustration of them.

Indeed, from the late eighties onwards, the economic benefits of local development stood out against the backdrop of globalisation and the rise of the knowledge-based economy. In political terms, progress in decentralisation, the success of the neo-liberal movement and new participatory democracy theories created conditions conducive to developing local endogenous potential. Strong support also came from most international organisations. However, despite the wealth of local initiatives, no firm foothold was established. Now, the bulk of financial and human resources are devoted to attracting foreign investment, with no thought for the potential harmful side-effects of a model of this kind. The reasons why local development has been sidelined when it seemed to show such promise for the future warrant detailed analysis. Are the games definitively over or is it possible to identify the means and avenues for potential reinvigoration to make our development more sustainable?

1.The beginning

1.1 Ineffective initial strategies for industrial change

The seventies and eighties were distinguished in Europe and the other developed countries by a series of sectoral crises which affected first conventional industries - mines, coal and steel, textiles - and then more recent industries - chemical, automotive and shipbuilding industries etc.

There were considerable job losses and the damage suffered by regions and cities was sometimes extreme (Commission, 2004). There was even talk of "disaster-stricken" regions at the time. Once the initial crisis had passed, it was frequently observed that operations to save firms in trouble or attempts to save jobs at all costs, in particular when it no longer made economic sense and in outdated production or operating conditions, were ineffective.

The need for strategies for change then became clear. The first of these strategies consisted of trying to find new investors who could create jobs for the unemployed in the area on a large scale. This approach was generally supported by both local public authorities and national governments, at great expense. All the funding and players possible were enlisted to make an area attractive. Two main tactics were used: retraining of staff made redundant and awarding of premiums, subsidies or tax exemption.

This path seemed attractive in the short term as it tended to give an area and numerous workers a new future quickly in economic conditions which were fairly similar to past conditions, with paid employment in the industrial sector. However, after a few years, this kind of strategy often proved disappointing for two reasons. Firstly, the system induced dishonest behaviour in premium-hunters who had little concern for the long-term viability of a project and very often pulled out once they had pocketed the premium. Secondly, the financial incentives artificially changed the profit conditions for a project and, once the subsidy period was over, the new firms would often disappear, dealing a second blow. Moreover, training efforts were often of no use because of the rapidly-changing needs of firms. The French regions Lorraine and Nord-Pas de Calais, and the East Midlands and Yorkshire in the United Kingdom experienced difficulties of this kind.

In the early nineties, the clear, often costly failure of these rein-dustrialisation projects was compared to two other, more modest strategies; these, however, yielded more lasting results. The first was anticipating the closure of a major factory by encouraging a myriad of small and medium-sized businesses, usually in the tertiary sector, to be set up in the area affected. The range of methods used included business incubators, spin-offs, outsourcing of non-core operations and clusters of local businesses. The second strategy aimed to gently change the focus of the local economy by drawing on the regions' resources and players, encouraging the establishment of projects run by the communities themselves with a view to more self-reliant development – the concept of developing local endogenous potential came into being. In both cases, the emphasis was on the new relationship between economy and region created by the development of services and the dissemination of information and communication technology.

These analyses were popularised in academic literature under the heading "new economic geography"; Porter (1998), Krugman (1991) and Venables (2005) are probably the best-known authors. Attempting to explain the reasons for ongoing disparities in regional development when new technology and the opening-up of world trade should have placed all regions on an equal footing, they identified the importance of non-physical growth factors present in places and societies. Thus, in the post-industrial era, the new assets of a region were no longer easy access to natural resources or location at waterway or other transport junctions so much as relationships of intellectual exchange and innovative stimulation forged between the business world, research centres or universities.

1.2 The benefits and components of local endogenous development

The new economic geography theories encourage public authorities to take more qualitative action as regards businesses and communities. For decision-makers it should be less important to try and graft activities from outside onto a region than to create a climate which will generate activities. It is a question of injecting a development process into environments which are already complex and "overcrowded" or, conversely, particularly ossified or resistant to innovation. This initiative requires opening-up of the local environment, exploitation of human resources and forging of partnerships.

In fact, taking the "invention-innovation-dissemination" sequence from the Schumpeterian cycle, it is precisely the dissemination phase which is weak in disadvantaged regions (Morgan, 2004). We have known for some years that research and development have beneficial effects which businesses have a tendency to internalise where public intervention is lacking. Public authorities must therefore ensure that a general environment is created which is conducive to disseminating innovation, encouraging in particular horizontal cooperation between economic players (businesses and research centres) located in a particular area rather than just vertical integration within a production chain.

Moreover, taking as a starting point the observation that the business establishment rate can vary from one to ten in a single country, depending on the region in question (DTI, 2002), a policy of cutting red tape and better regulation at European or national level is not enough. It must be supplemented by specific measures to promote entrepreneurship and support the growth of existing businesses, gearing advice or support services supplied to local or regional needs.

As this phenomenon took hold in developed countries, in regions affected by industrial crises or in depopulated rural areas, it was given the name "redevelopment" (Greffe, 1992). It consisted of drawing on new growth factors (knowledge, confidence, network cooperation, investment in organisation) or combining the old factors (land, capital, labour) differently, of revealing an area's hidden potential and converting it into economic assets, developing the area's specific characteristics. Geographical proximity took on particular importance as it determined the possibilities of physical interaction between people, interaction which was of prime importance in establishing and maintaining the quality of these invisible factors. Action and analysis thus took should take place at sub-regional level.

Politically, local development quickly became seen as a sure means of diagnosing the real problems in a region or in a group in difficulties, developing solutions to these problems, creating a feeling of belonging and securing lasting results. On a wider note, it enabled deprived inner-cities, small rural municipalities and micro-regions, step by step, to take control of their future once again (Jouen, 2004 a).

Local development, partnership and bottom-up approach emerged as a new way of governing at a time when neo-liberal thought was prevailing (Loughlin, 2000). It was an auxiliary response to market failures when public authorities were pulling out. This trend tallied with the theory that the state's standard, expensive interventions were unable to resolve increasingly complex problems and to meet increasingly specific individual demands. As free competition brought major social and regional imbalances, remedies from both private and public local players were necessary. Thus, calls for new, more efficient governance went hand in hand with pushes towards decentralisation, with local and regional actors given greater responsibility in running projects and managing financing (Calame, 2003). Contracts and partnerships were to take the place of the old hierarchical methods.

Thus, the need for both political and economic efficiency prompted residents and players in an area to come together to take decisions and sometimes implement projects, using various participatory democracy methods (Donzelot & Epstein, 2006).

1.3 Support from international organisations

One after the other, all the international organisations acknowledged the importance of decentralisation and grass-roots action in the development process. The OECD was the first, with the LEED (*Local Economic and Employment Development)* programme, which it is still running, just over 20 years on. This programme, backed by a small group of supporters from the majority of the OECD member states, added a training centre at the beginning of the century in Trento (Italy), in one of the recognised cradles of social enterprise. Its activities take the form of seminars and exchanges of expertise in five areas: jobs and skills, entrepreneurship, globalisation, governance and social innovation.

The European institutions' interest in local development dates back to 1984, when the Council adopted a Resolution on the Contribution of Local Employment Initiatives to Combating Unemployment (Council, 1984). It was after 1993, however, with the White Paper on Growth, Competitiveness and Employment (Commission, 1993), drafted at a time of high unemployment, that European policy promoting local employment initiatives really gained a high profile (Commission, 1995).

Over the following five years, numerous programmes were launched on the basis of regular evaluation reports (Commission, 1995 b, 1996, 1998). Almost all the European summits referred to them in the official conclusions, culminating in the inclusion of specific guidelines in the European Employment Strategy and subsequently the Lisbon Strategy in 2000 (Jouen, 2004 b).

The 2000-2006 Structural Funds programming period played a key role in the development of local endogenous development, with European Social Fund resources targeting jobs and social cohesion and European Regional Development Fund resources for enterprise and innovation. However, the adoption of the Communication on Strengthening the local dimension of the European Employment Strategy (2001) unexpectedly marked the climax of this trend, which rapidly lost momentum over the following months.

The World Bank took the same approach with its 1997 annual report, calling for decentralisation and "good governance", which were presented as essential if the funds and programmes operating in the least-developed countries were to be efficient and effective. Indeed, this political line bore the mark of direct intellectual influence from its vice-chairman and chief economist, who made no bones about the fact that participation and appropriation by local communities was crucial and appealed for more community-led local development (Stiglitz, 1998).

The International Monetary Fund may well have been the last on the list, as it was late 1999 before it published an official analysis on the merits of decentralised governance (Dillinger, 1999).

Within the UN's sphere of influence, the establishment of the Millennium Goals helped to popularise the concept of local development although it was systematically presented as an instrument geared to disadvantaged countries, regions or communities. Thus, the ILO set up a database on Poverty, Local

Development and Decent Work and supported a programme known as Delnet for training those involved in local development in poor countries.

A number of United Nations agencies (UNDP, UNESCO, WHO, UNICEF, HCR etc.) acknowledging the benefits of a regional approach to development, started to coordinate to deliver a consistent message to governments receiving aid and plan to make this initiative formal in an agreement which would allow the regional dimension to be promoted in future reforms of the UN system. Specifically, the UNDP has been supporting the ART (Appui aux réseaux territoriaux – local network support) programme for developing decentralised cooperation since 2005.

1.4 A new era approaches

As regards theoretical analysis, interest in local endogenous development came from various groups, all concerned about the social, economic and political consequences of globalisation arising from the dissemination of communication technology.

In Europe, local development strategies revealed the potential of new tertiary sectors for job creation, particularly related to culture, the environment, leisure, health and education (Jouen, 2000 b). They also brought to light the original formulas for co-financing or hybridisation between the public and private sectors (Laville & Eme, 1994). The reflection on new forms of entrepreneurship in a post-industrial context revealed the quantitative and qualitative importance of a non-profit-making intermediary economy, termed "third-sector" (Lipietz, 2001) or "social economy" (Borzaga & Defourny, 2001). Local development was seen as a means of breaking away from "profitability at any price" and restoring the room for manoeuvre of people, residents and workers.

As regards the regions, the range of possible futures for rural areas or disadvantaged urban districts became considerably wider, helping to meet a growing need for differentiation between individuals and communities at a time when the public financing which was a feature of our contemporary societies was undergoing radical cuts. It is no great surprise that the values generally upheld by local development initiatives tallied with those known as "post-modern" values (Jouen, 2000 a).

Faced with world competition, local development seemed to some to be the last bastion against the fickle global economy (Rodrik, 1997), whereas others welcomed the flexibility it gave regions, enabling them to negotiate with the prevailing economy. This latter combination was popularised by the newly-coined term "glo-cal" and the slogan "Think global, act local".

At the end of the nineties, the conditions therefore seemed to be in place for the economy of the 21st Century, drawing fully on the technological and communication revolution, to strike out, step by step, along the path of sustainable development and show a return on local endogenous development strategies (Robin, 1989).

2.The present situation

It must be said that the beginning of the century has not witnessed the widespread dissemination of development that is self-driven, partnership and bottom-up approach, but has instead re-launched competition between cities or regions in the name of an intensified globalisation.

2.1 Expansion of the concentration – agglomeration phenomenon

The principal trend in Europe over the last fifteen years has been the polarisation of territorial development, following a "hubs and spokes" pattern or an "archipelago" pattern (Viard, 1994). This evolution, which covers the whole planet and has gathered pace recently with the spread of communication technologies and the reorganisation of companies' production methods, has its own distinct form in Europe. The phenomenon of "global convergence, local divergence" can be seen at ever lower levels (Jouen, 2001).

Thus, while the Commission welcomes a certain convergence between countries in its regular reports on economic and social cohesion, it has to concede that inequalities between the regions persist and in some cases are deepening. There is no doubt that over the last ten years the share of Community GDP provided by the traditional economic "core" bounded by London, Paris, Milan, Munich and Hamburg, has shrunk, but it is only the capital regions of other countries that have profited and not secondary regional centres (Commission, 2007a).

This concentration is explained by what economists refer to as positive externalities, the product of localised social interactions which have a beneficial impact on productivity. Agglomeration phenomena are cumulative and based on both migration of labour and the relocation of companies. In contrast to what happens in the United Sates, the geographical mobility of Europeans remains structurally weak and cannot serve to mitigate disparities. At the regional level, this movement is magnified by the grouping of dynamic companies keen to cut their transaction costs and to spread out the repercussions of their investments and their technological progress, while maintaining a well trained local labour force (Veltz, 2002).

We are witnessing, then, a polarisation between regions which have a heavy concentration of companies with high profit margins and salaries and regions with poor productivity and a low-skilled workforce which can only compete by undercutting. This puts them in direct competition with less developed countries and makes them vulnerable in the process of trade globalisation.

The difficulties encountered by the industrial sector in Portugal at the beginning of the century – facing competition from the output of central European countries and much less attractive for foreign investments – is a perfect illustration of this phenomenon. The country would have had to carry out quickly conversion towards sectors with higher value added and to redouble its training and investment efforts in research-development. However, the positive result would not have been obtained for the whole country.

The exacerbation of the central-peripheral regional divide in Europe has been helped by the improvement of transport infrastructures and the advances of the single market (Martin, 1999). The introduction of Economic and Monetary Union has helped the trend along. European integration has made it possible to cut product distribution costs considerably and so given investors the chance to choose the most suitable location from the whole of Europe, free from physical, and above all regulatory, constraints that have traditionally burdened cross border transit.

This trend has opened the way for the less developed or the most remote countries to catch up quickly, enabling them to make the most of their comparative advantages and to profit from the "territorial indetermination" (Morgan, 2001) created by the exogenous shock from the arrival of new information and communication technologies. Thus, Ireland and Finland have become attractive in new niches. For its part, the growth registered in the last ten years by the vast border area at the heart of Europe including some parts of the Czech Republic, Poland, Slovakia and Austria is fuelled by another logic: the automotive industry's need for geographical concentration.

On the other hand, some regions and cities appear incapable of – or dilatory in – profiting from the new wave of technological innovation. Their failures are cumulative and as much cultural as economic and social. The causes one could cite include: political structures inherited from the past, remoteness from big consumer markets and transport costs, traditional inequalities between town and country, a sluggish economic environment, scarcity of human resources, inflexible labour markets and, more particularly, the unit labour cost. In addition to weak productivity and a poorly skilled workforce, regions that lag behind also suffer from underuse of local resources due to failures on the part of public institutions. Thus even if, for a few years in Western Europe, the rural areas have been seeing flowing new inhabitants and business entrepreneurs, the constraint remains high in terms of qualification level of labour force. The small companies located in a rural environment or in low population density areas are handicapped by a less stimulating climate (Jarvis et al., 2006)

Also regrettable in some cases is the poor coordination between Community and national sectoral policies. Moreover, the progress made by the single market and transport systems has helped to change local consumption patterns and brought them into line with those of the wealthiest regions. Suddenly, peripheral zones have become more dependent on consumer goods and services originating outside.

The growth experienced by the most central regions and countries often derives from their capacity to make the most of their intangible assets. One of the keys of their ability to adapt is what is termed "social capital" (Putnam, 1993), which involves public authorities as well as the public and economic players. Its richness is the result of sound interplay between the social and the economic, i.e., a highly skilled workforce, relations between universities, research centres and units of production, a climate of cooperation between businesses, a decent quality of life guaranteed by efficient public services, and the integrity and dynamism of public authorities. Densely populated cities and areas have traditionally been better placed because they offer businesses both a large consumer market and a large and diverse labour force. Industrial districts and clusters are the archetype of this form of rapid-growth development that is very attractive to new businesses and those with high added value. As for the enormous interest such centres are currently attracting in Europe, this quite simply represents the mobilisation of local resources to the benefit of exogenous development.

2.2 The prosperity of the development model based on foreign direct investment

Reflection and action regarding the attractiveness strategies have been given a boost with the arrival on the scene of India for information technologies and of China for everything else, with their capacity not only to offer gigantic markets for European exporters, but also to install themselves in developed countries, conduct development strategies at world level and to compete with our economies thanks to wages which are one tenth of those in the developed economies.

After some years in the doldrums, international investment flows have returned to growth (UNCTAD, 2006). In 2006, they reached USD 1 230 billion, with the EU-27 receiving half and the USA 14% (65% for developed countries). Several specific factors have played a part in this growth in international investment: the continuing opening-up of national economies to foreign capital, the swift development of new sectors (such as biotechnologies and the environment) at international level, the growing power of the multinationals of emerging countries, and the increasing role of new forms of investment and financing.

Over the last five years, the "market" of internationally mobile investment in Europe has been responsible for 2 800 projects and the creation of at least

180000 jobs each year. As to the nature of the jobs created, most investment is in production projects and, more particularly, in manufacturing industry (78%), and the automotive and electronic equipment sectors. Recently, commercial and logistics services have given rise to FDI that has created jobs. This "market" has a dual structure: on the one hand, it has some large-scale projects, each providing more than 500 jobs, and, on the other, a myriad of small projects, often involving the services sector, that create fewer than a hundred jobs and often a few dozen at most.

It is European companies that feed most of the FDI flow (55%), while Asian businesses account for only a marginal share (16%). The nature of FDI very much depends on the countries of origin and destination and on the sectors; their contrasting profiles reveal the different localisation strategies of multinationals (Jouen et al., 2003). They take advantage of the low production costs in central or eastern European countries by locating labour operations there; they seek to gain market access and to profit from the skills in the countries of western Europe by establishing R&D centres, logistics and distribution centres or headquarters there (Hatem, 2007).

Thus, regions and towns enter a beauty contest orchestrated by companies on the one hand and national or supranational governments on the other. The success of a forum such as the La Baule World Investment Conference, devoted exclusively to the competitiveness of territories and regional attractiveness, is a perfect illustration of this. For five years now, it has brought together almost a thousand people and more than a hundred directors of large companies. Imitating the British, French, Irish or Swedish models, the countries of central and eastern Europe are not to be outdone (e.g. Czech Invest, PAIilZ, ITDH). For some years now, local and regional export-support and investment agencies have been multiplying.

Massive public and private funding is devoted to analysing how attractive countries or regions are (e.g. the French Agency AFII). Every year, internationally renowned bodies work out specific indicators to serve as a reference for foreign investors and their bankers: AT Kearney and its globalisation index, the World Economic Forum and its business competitiveness index, IMD and its index of global competitiveness, and the World Investment Report.

2.3 The exhaustion or "hijacking" of local endogenous development

When it comes to territorialised development, we are witnessing a decoupling of local endogenous development and local economic development.

The former, which includes a strong social element involving a bottom-up partnership-based approach, is enlisted to solve the problems of a marginalised section of the population or territory. Although political and public decision-makers frequently use this as a tool of governance – to ensure the support of the public and other local players –, it has every semblance of a "low-cost" option or a "last chance" solution for all those who are incapable of facing up to market competition. In this respect, the European trend is in line with the line taken by international organisations and UN agencies.

The questions that were once entertained about the influence of local endogenous development on the prevailing development model no longer (for the moment?) have any point. All that is achieved is a slight shifting of the borders between the private sector and the protected public sector – agreed to even by the champions of local endogenous development, who then talk of a "plural economy" (Sauvage, 1996) – and local endogenous development is relegated to the wings in the name of cohesion and solidarity. It is acknowledged as a complementary strategy, more effective and less costly than resorting to entirely public funding for the "rejects" of the real economy. It claims little capital or material resources, but in turn produces limited results.

Local or regional economic development has taken a very different trajectory, having to some degree supported and reinforced exogenous growth. In fact, it very quickly became clear that in order to stimulate regional growth, FDI should produce "external economies" – i.e., they should lead to improvements in what was on offer locally, in technical skills and network activities. Only when a region is capable of advantageously developing a strong complementarity between FDI and the innovation process can such investments significantly affect regional growth (Riou, 2003).

Unlike models of exogenous growth, which insisted on a rapid adjustment to technological shocks, the "new growth" models seek to make technological progress endogenous by linking it more closely with investment decisions about human capital and the improvement of skills (Morgan, 2001). Although R&D expenditure is high, it accounts for only a small part of the innovation process and the most effective intervention policy at regional level is to step up the dissemination and transfer of technology.

In political discourse, this movement has manifested itself at European level in the progressive toughening of the Lisbon Strategy, launched in 2000. Over the years, on the pretext of rationalisation, most of the recommendations concerning local development have been dropped. An additional stage has been embarked upon in which cohesion policy has acquired new directions and a goal of "regional competitiveness" to match the established one of "convergence", together with a precise targeting of regional expenditure.

The results have surpassed expectations, since EUR 200 billion out of the EUR 347.4 billion provided for cohesion policy in 2007-2013 will in effect be devoted to competitiveness. Commissioner Hübner was upbeat in March 2007 at the First International Convention for a Regional and Local Approach to Development, saying "today regional policy is not only about internal convergence; it is also an essential lever for stimulating global competitiveness across the EU at regional and local level".

In France, while the triennial public budget for supporting "competitiveness centres" amounts to EUR 1.5 billion, an envelope of EUR 400 million has been released under the European Social Fund for endogenous local development for seven years.

At the end of the day, local development could be considered a victim of its own success, "hijacked" by the dominant economic model. By introducing the notion of competitiveness, this model has managed to appropriate for the ends of competition the intangible factors of territorial dynamism, or to tip social solidarity and collective fulfilment into the mercantile world.

3. Reasons

Instead of a paradigm shift brought about by the recognition of its benefits, we have seen a marginalisation of endogenous local development. There are a number of possible explanations for this, some relating to the weaknesses of local endogenous development itself and others to the strength of the exogenous model of development. The latter include both economic and more political or ideological reasons.

3.1 The intrinsic weaknesses of endogenous local development

Local development is still essentially an empirical practice and, although research has been conducted in this area, there is still a dearth of conceptual tools. From a theoretical perspective, its detractors make no bones about stating that "*there is no agreed generic definition of local development in either the academic or the political and administrative literature*" (Davezies & Estèbe, 2007). Without adding to the polemic, it must be acknowledged that, more than ten years after the first attempts to establish a regulatory framework or standardise certain methods, the same failings persist. Building on and transposing successful experiences remains problematic, since the human dimension and the skills and capacities of the individual people behind local initiatives play a crucial part in that success.

In fact, beneath the overarching term 'local development', two different approaches can be distinguished: the first is socio-political and focuses predominantly on local groups' autonomy and capacity for self-organisation; the second is linked to the field of socio-economics and the attempts to formulate an alternative to the dominant economy. This ambivalent combination of social and economic approaches is probably a pitfall, in that it gives rise to different and sometimes contradictory expectations.

Decisions and preferences are still influenced by historical, geographic and cultural factors. Endogenous local development is ascribed different places in different countries depending on the role played by the welfare state. In the Scandinavian countries, characterised by a high degree of egalitarianism and cohesion, it is still in its infancy since the dominant model is intolerant of experiments at the periphery. In the Anglo-Saxon countries, which are more individualistic and liberal but nevertheless open to community-based approaches, endogenous development is often equated with a search for local or regional identity. In north-western Europe, where the state still plays the role of policeman and tries to use legislation to redefine the limits between the public and private spheres, including for businesses and families, it is doing relatively well. Lastly, in some Mediterranean countries and the countries in the former communist bloc, the underdevelopment of organised civil society and the practical difficulties around partnership act as brakes on local development.

Thus, the complexity of the concept, connected with the existence of different approaches and the impossibility of establishing a "pure" model has hampered wider dissemination of endogenous development beyond a narrow circle of cognoscenti. The fact that endogenous development is closely bound up with the public authorities also makes it vulnerable to both budgetary restrictions and political trends. It has a difficult path to trace between the private and public sectors, and does not always manage to avoid the temptation of clientelism.

The term "disappointment" may seem exaggerated, but it is nonetheless comprehensible, since in some quarters the expectations of this approach may have been too high, being presented as a substitute for the growth experienced during the 30 boom years following World War II. This dashed hope probably had more to do with a nostalgic dream than with a realistic understanding of the new globalised economic system.

3.2 The economic reasons

If we compare the economic performance of the two models, the verdict is unambiguous. Various local authorities have noted, with some bitterness: "*It is probably impossible to succeed using endogenous development alone. Those mountain regions which have been successful are accessible and, in some cases, even major European hubs*" (AEM, 2007).

However, in practice, this kind of comparison is equivalent to weighing an investment in the tourism industry intended to create several dozen or even hundred jobs within the space of a few months, against an initiative to diversify rural tourism that may only generate one or two jobs, perhaps only part-time jobs for people already involved. In view of the low numbers and the time taken to produce results, political and business circles would no doubt judge the endogenous development project to have produced negligible durable benefits.

The most recent European studies (Blonström, 2006) confirm that FDI (foreign direct investment) has a positive impact on productivity in the host regions as well as on their capacity to deal with global competition, without producing a significant negative impact on labour demand. As far as productivity is concerned, the results of FDI are generally above the norm and improve the regional average (for example, by around 50% in manufacturing industry in the new Member States).

Moreover, they have a spill-over effect on the productivity of the local enterprises they deal with (by up to 40%). FDI brings new technologies, new know-how and new managerial skills. In France, one out of four new jobs is created through international investment and one in seven jobs is linked to existing FDI. In Europe, it is estimated that FDI accounts for an average of 10% of total annual public and private-sector expenditure on R&D and for as much as 20% in some countries (Hatem, 2007).

For its part, endogenous local development is characterised by slow returns on investment and weak capacity to generate profits. It takes five or ten years for this form of development to produce results, the time required for mentalities to evolve and structural changes to take place in the environment. There are no economies of scale and it generates little added value, hence its ongoing need for external financing. Moreover, the argument in favour of local development hinges on a cost comparison between the jobs it generates and jobs in the public sector (Jouen, 2000 a).

It also has very high requirements in terms of staff and immaterial factors, at a time when the ageing of the population and the constraints of economic efficiency incline towards substituting labour with capital. Lastly, this kind of development is largely based on short production-consumption loops and local consumption, which puts it at the opposite end of the spectrum from the dominant economic interests. After all, the accepted wisdom amongst economic forecasters is that any country whose growth is based solely on domestic production and consumption is in a precarious situation. All this aside, the lack of adequate statistical instruments or indicators, particularly with respect to cost-benefit analysis, makes it difficult to measure the performance of local development (Grasland & Hamez, 2005).

The fact that Europe's political decision-makers have opted to attract businesses to poor or declining regions rather than to push workers towards growth regions can also be explained by default. In so doing, they accept the consequences of people's extreme unwillingness to move to look for work, in contrast to the United States. This is in part legitimate, since the culture and sociological obstacles inherent in our continent's diversity are not likely to disappear in the near future (Martin, 2001). Conversely, low mobility can be perceived as an advantage since it allows the creation of a strong local identity and builds a region's social capital. This analysis seems to be shared by the European Commissioner, Janez Potocnik, who sees FDI as "*a shield against the brain drain*".

3.3 The political reasons

The third set of explanations is political or even ideological in nature. Indeed, globalisation is as much a cultural as an economic or financial phenomenon and holds a great fascination for our societies. Chancellor Angela Merkel went so far as to state, at the World Economic Forum in 2007, that, "*globalisation is a process of liberation*". Although it does lay down a number of conditions, UNCTAD considers international trade to be a crucial factor in growth and progress (UNCTAD, 2007). In contrast, endogenous local development simply claims to help people to take their fate into their own hands and enable them to improve the conditions in which they live.

From the perspective of political sociology, development through globalisation is the easy way, whereas endogenous development requires "public virtue". Its practitioners recognise that they may well be asking too much from the local populations who are supposed to organise themselves, in that, unlike the other development strategies which merely ask people to buy or consume, they require the inhabitants to make a personal and collective commitment (McInroy, 2004). Furthermore, local development comes up against the same obstacles as participatory or grassroots democracy initiatives, where lack of skills, time and will result in limited participation and hence to questions about or challenges to their legitimacy (Mothé, 2006).

The recent academic literature still contains virulent critiques such as the following: "*It is as if the combination of the concepts of political self-government and re-balancing has resulted in the establishment of a kind of general right to development, which has led to competition (between regions) being confused with competitiveness (at national level). The leaven for this general right to development is the concept of "endogenous development" [...]. Not all development problems can be resolved at regional level. For this reason, we must move away from a territorial approach to development. The future for local development does not lie in contracts or project proposals, but in building partnerships for initiatives of regional and national interest between the State, the regions and the major cities." (Davezies & Estèbe, 2007).* Although, the rhetoric may initially seem impressive, a deeper analysis of the argument shows that it is actually about refusing to give any actors besides nation states the right to play a role in economic development. To find this attitude expressed in 2007, in Europe, is surprising, since it is tantamount to denying the obvious. However, this very relentlessness demonstrates the quasi-ideological nature of the confrontation. It becomes still more interesting once we start exploring the avenues that might make our development model more sustainable.

4.Possible ways forward

In the medium term, endogenous development does not seem to offer an alternative to FDI strategies. Anyhow, the developed countries need to continue to be driven by sustained growth and the capacity of our development model to exploit new intangible factors is a sign of its vitality. In the longer term, however, the prospects are less benign, as attested by the repeated warnings about the state of the natural environment, the fragility of the financial system or the risks of conflicts induced by growing disparities in development, made much more perceptible by instantaneous communication. Against this background, it is possible that local endogenous development has not had its last word.

4.1 The limits of exogenous development

Is the purpose of local endogenous development merely to fuel the competitiveness of regions and provide input to FDI strategies? Yes, would reply, without hesitation, those who adhere to the recommendations of the "new economic geography" theorists. This means that in Europe, within the framework of the Lisbon Strategy, each region is expected to embark on a benchmarking exercise in order to identify optimal performance and then attempt to achieve it.

However, this conception of regional development and of the role of local authorities in it is not shared unanimously. Some experts feel that European regions and cities have other roles to play in the spatial division of labour, such as taking part in the race towards "the best knowledge-based economy in the world" (Bell, 2004). Local and regional authorities may quite legitimately reject such a proposal or be unable to compete with the best, to the point where they opt for another way. Moreover, some small prosperous areas may succeed in extricating themselves from global competition by adopting a niche strategy or by mitigating its harmful effects.

Also of concern is the fact that the Lisbon Strategy could move towards a model which does not recognise the basic European values of difference – linguistic, cultural, behavioural, moral and philosophical – and extreme regional diversity. After all, the most advanced stage of the knowledge-based economy calls for a far more sophisticated and flexible vision of the needs of people and regions and of what they can contribute in a Europe of 27.

Another question may arise concerning the consequences of mobilising all forces which contribute to the social dynamic (culture, education, environment, etc) of a region and help to increase its appeal. In fact, such a process leads to a gradual shift away from strategies geared to attracting investment to strategies designed to attract talent, which may turn out to be a bad policy at local, national and European levels. It could culminate in the replacement of the much disparaged "foot-loose companies" by "foot-loose workers" – kinds of mercenaries of the knowledge-based economy. What guarantee is there that these talented people, conscious of their value and hyper-mobile, would not, after a short while, accept a more attractive offer from another region? How strong would be their attachment to their new job or new home in relation to the promise of an increase in their skills, their quality of life or their income? Fostering a "brain drain" like the one which Ireland currently does vis-à-vis Poland or the Baltic States does not have anything special to recommend it either. It is a zero sum game at EU level, a deadweight loss at national or regional level. In the final analysis, it is not only about having to attract people to a locality but also knowing how to keep them there so that they create wealth by settling locally. This reaffirms the importance of local endogenous development, no longer simply as a factor improving the appeal of a locality but also as factor promoting socialisation, personal fulfilment and cultural enrichment.

Sociologists and geographers never cease to warn us about the risks of social disorder or "conflicts of civilisations" that we run if we remain indifferent to demands by the excluded to be afforded new opportunities (Bauman, 1999). International organisations are trying to respond to this by rightly advocating the idea of local endogenous development, which makes it possible to bring about a transition in the context of a "protected" economy, a factor making for diversity but also innovation. In developed countries, and in particular the EU, the negative externalities of concentration are now officially recognised (Nordregio, 2007).

Traditionally, the argument for cohesion policy has rested on the need to prevent regions or social groups from lagging behind, as this is a factor liable to curb overall European growth. Now the argument has been broadened to cover environmental damage and adverse territorial effects, such as the higher cost of housing, the reduction in the space available for commercial activity, traffic congestion and pollution (Commission, 2007 b). The extension of this model to the whole planet has negative repercussions for health, the exhaustion of energy resources and the environment more generally, as documented in a number of particularly worrying reports, such as those of the IPCC.

In essence, the problem derives from the exclusive nature of FDI Strategies and their propensity to "swallow up" everything else. To function effectively our economies need a certain degree of diversity to enable them to absorb any exogenous shocks but also to mitigate negative externalities. By analogy with the natural sciences, which recognise the importance of the biodiversity for maintaining balance in a living environment, local development can be considered to play a key role in eco-diversity.

It is useful here to revisit the writings of the French historian Fernand Braudel, who described the economy as the construction of an edifice with several storeys, each corresponding to different levels of commercial and human exchange. The prosperity of the whole is determined by the balance between the various storeys and good communication between them. In this model, some economic activities attributable to local development are present on several storeys, complementing rather than serving those activities which are the outcome of exogenous development (Jouen, 2000 a).

4.2 Re-exploring the possibilities

The experience of the past twenty years shows that it is illusory to think that local endogenous development can co-exist alongside exogenous development without deliberate intervention. Such intervention can take various forms, ranging from regulation to financial support, from the setting of rules to the use of contracts. It may be public, but also private, or, then again, reflect the views of civil society. It must, in all cases, be founded on the emerging dynamics, with a view to re-exploring the possibilities for different categories of territory, segments of the population and types of economic activity.

Some of the possibilities can be outlined here, drawing on examples which are beginning to be known, without, however, having been properly exploited to date.

Decision-makers and local and regional players could be made more aware of the existence of three significantly different types of clustering governance (Perrat & Zinneman, 2003): one consistent with agglomeration, based on the spatial concentration of heterogeneous economic activities with no links between them; another consistent with specialisation, where there is a dominant industrial activity or product in which a whole range of players is involved; and a third consistent with specification, where different types of coordination between players make it possible not only to enjoy a sustainable competitive advantage in an activity but also to move into a new activity in the event of a sectoral crisis.

Whilst the first two of these strategies are widespread, the third is less so. However, specification seems the most promising since it generates strong externalities and shows little vulnerability. It draws its strength from certain components of endogenous development, since it implies working around a body of specific resources accumulated in a particular region and trying to strengthen the capacity of individuals and companies to redeploy (Bouba-Olga, 2007).

In another vein, recent analyses provide updates on the new consumption opportunities related to information and communication technologies. These make it possible, at global level, to aggregate demands which are very marginal in quantitative terms, thus making it profitable to sell and manufacture products which had earlier been abandoned because the market for them was too small. Hence they also afford opportunities for products or services which previously did not have the financial means to gain access to large markets on account of the screening practices of traditional retail chains. Finally, they make it possible to lengthen the life of products and thus to smooth demand. These new circumstances, called the "long tail" phenomenon, open up opportunities not only in the tourist and cultural fields, but also for niche products (food products of the type PDO/PGI, craft products, luxury products). It also makes products and services accessible in remote areas. Producers, like consumers, could find this phenomenon interesting, as it does not require additional marketing costs (Anderson, 2007).

Similarly, the relocalisation of the economy, although frequently advocated, still remains very much a slogan. To give it real political legitimacy, there is a need to develop a consistent, offensive argument, press ahead with the analysis of the negative externalities of agglomerations and adopt a statistical system that goes beyond the UNDP indicators. This option should also be backed up by a wide range of legal and financial instruments to promote regional authenticity, embracing quality, security and proximity.

Another possible way forward starts from the "residential dynamic" that was identified by a group working under the auspices of the Commission of the National Plan (Mouhoud, 2006). Urban sprawl, "rurbanisation" and the influx of people to coastal zones and sun-belt areas point to reasons for mobility other than employment, particularly in connection with the advent of the services society and demographic ageing. These new circumstances provide economic justification for local or regional public policies which are not geared merely towards attracting companies but also to improving living conditions (housing, environment, public services, etc.). They open the way to intervention of various kinds focusing on enhancing local endogenous potential capable of checking transport movements and mitigating pressures on land and the environment caused by agglomeration.

If we take the argument a step further, it is possible to find the foundations of a new theory of local development. We have seen how interest in endogenous development grew out of industrial crises and the fight against unemployment. Job creation and the pursuit of local solidarity against the background of the decline of the welfare state therefore provided a platform for the renaissance of the local dimension in the early 1980s.

With the advance of individualism, we have to recognise that not only have considerations related to competition and performance in the world of work permeated all of our social relations (Honneth, 2006) but also that socialisation through work has lost vigour. Thus, we can postulate that the loss of impetus in local endogenous development and its progressive containment in the social field at the turn of the century are also the result of generational renewal and a certain lack of interest among the general public.

Consequently, the local dynamic has to be rebuilt on new ground, on the basis of the willingness to live together, place of residence and local services. This is a narrow way as the shift towards consumerism will offer little help and the call for responsible citizenship, though more promising, remains somewhat of a gamble.

Finally, underlying the scope left for local endogenous development by FDI strategies looms the question of whether our model of development has the capacity to become more sustainable, in terms of non-waste of natural and human resources, preservation of the environment and reducing tensions and conflicts of all kinds. The next twenty years will be a testing time for the whole of mankind.

Literature

AEM – Association européenne des élus de montagne (2007) *Contribution pour l'agenda territorial de l'Union européenne* – non papier

Anderson Ch. (2007) *La longue traîne*, Editions Village mondial

Barry F. & Bradley J. (1997) "FDI and trade: the Irish host-country experience" in *Royal economic society economic journal* 107, pp 1798-1811

Bauman Z. (1999) *Le coût humain de la mondialisation* Editions Hachette littératures, Paris

Bell J. (2004) "Réflexions sur l'approche ascendante à partir de la pratique" in *Développement local, partenariat et approche ascendante: où en sommes-nous maintenant?* Jouen M. Ed, Séminaire n°21 - Notre Europe & ECOTEC (www.notre-europe.eu)

Blomström M. (2006) *Study on FDI and regional development*, Copenhagen Economics, European Commission (DG REGIO)

Borzaga C. & Defourny J. (2001) *The emergence of social enterprise*, Routledge London

Bouba-Olga O. (2007) "Délocalisation et désindustrialisation: que peuvent les collectivités territoriales?" in *Pouvoirs locaux* n°72, Paris

Calame P. (2003) *La démocratie en miettes – Pour une révolution de la gouvernance*, Editions Descartes & Cie, Paris

Castells M. (1996), *The rise of the network society* , Blackwell Publisher, Oxford

Castells M. (1997) *The power of identity* , Blackwell Publisher, Oxford

Combes P. P. & Laforucade M. (2000) "transportation costs decline and regional inequalities: evidence from France 1978-1993" mimeo CERAS-ENPC

Davezies L. & Estebe Ph. (2007) "L'autonomie politique dans l'interdépendance économique?" in *Pouvoirs locaux* n°72

Davezies L. & Veltz P. (2006) "Les métamorphoses du territoire: nouvelles mobilités, nouvelles inégalités" in La République des idées – Le Monde, Paris

Defourny J., Favreau L., Laville J-L. & Spear R. (Eds) (2001) *Tackling social exclusion in Europe, the contribution of the social economy*, Ashgate

Dillinger W. & Fay M. (1999) "From centralized to decentralized governance" in vol.36 n°4 *Finance & Development* (quaterly magazine of the IMF)

Donzelot J. et Epstein R. (2006) "Démocratie et participation: l'exemple de la rénovation urbaine" in Revue Esprit, n°7, Paris

DTI (2002) "Small Business and government – the way forward", Small business service Department of Trade and Industry, UK Government

European Commission (1993), *Growth, Competitiveness, Employment – Challenges and tracks for the XXIst century* OPOCE supplément 6/93C

European Commission (1995), Communication "A European strategy for the Local Development and Employment Initiatives" COM (95) 273

European Commission (1995), *The Local Development and Employment Initiatives, an inquiry in the European Union,* SEC 95-564

European Commission (1996), *Lessons for territorial and local employments pacts, First report on Local Development and Employment Initiatives,* EC Working Paper, OPOCE, CE 07 97 272 FR;

European Commission (1998), *The era of tailor-made jobs, Second report on Local Development and Employment Initiatives,* EC Working Paper, OPOCE, CE 09 97 220 FR

European Commission (2001), Communication "Reinforce the local dimension of the European Employment Strategy" COM (2001) 629

European Commission (2004), Communication "Accompagner les mutations structurelles: une politique industrielle pour l'Europe élargie" (tableau sur la désindustrialisation), COM (2004) 274

European Commission (2007), Communication "Fourth Report on Economic ans Social Cohesion", COM (2007)273

European Commission (2007) " Fourth Report on Economic and Social Cohesion – Growing Regions, Growing Europe"

European Council (1984), Council Resolution n.161/01 June 7th 1984

Favreau L. & Frechette L. (2002) *Mondialisation, économie sociale, développement local et solidarité internationale* , Presses de l'université du Québec

Fujita M., Krugman P., & Venables A. (1999) *The spatial economy: cities, regions and international trade*, MIT Press, Cambridge MA

Grasland C. et Hamez G (2005) "Vers la construction d'un indicateur de cohésion territoriale" in *L'espace géographique* n°2 pp97-116

Greffe X. (1992), *Sociétés post-industrielles et redéveloppement*, Collection Pluriel Hachette, Paris

GIEC – IPCC (2007) *Climate change 2007*, Working Groups Reports only available (www.ipcc.ch)

Hatem F. (2007) "Les grandes tendances des investissements internationaux en Europe: une analyse à partir des bases de données AFII pour la période 2002-2006" in *Les Notes Bleues de Bercy* n°324, Paris

Honneth A.(2006) *La société du mépris, vers une nouvelle théorie critique*, La découverte, Paris

Jarvis D., Dunham Ph. & Ilbery Br. (2006) "Local rural labour markets: enterprising or constraining?" in *Local economy* vol. 21, n°2

Jouen M. (2000), *Diversité européenne, mode d'emploi*, Editions Descartes et Cie, Paris

Jouen M. (2000), *L'action de l'Union européenne en faveur des emplois d'initiative locale*, "Problématiques européennes" n°6 - Notre Europe (février 2000) (www.notre-europe.eu)

Jouen M. (2001) *Comment renforcer la cohésion économique et sociale après 2006 ?* Séminaire du 23 mai 2001 - Notre Europe (www.notre-europe.eu)

Jouen M., Moutier S. & Welsch K. (2003) "Cinq petites Europe, des flux commerciaux recomposés", in *Le Courrier des pays de l'Est* n°1039

Jouen M. (2004) *Développement local, partenariat et approche ascendante: où en sommes-nous maintenant?* Séminaire n°21 – Notre Europe & ECOTEC (www.notre-europe.eu)

Jouen M. (2004) "La stratégie européenne pour l'emploi local" in *L'Europe sans Bruxelles, une analyse de la méthode ouverte de coordination,* Dehousse R. (Ed), L'Harmattan, Paris,

Krugman P. (1991) *Geography and trade*, MIT Press, Cambridge MA

Laville J-L. & Eme B. (Eds) (1994) *Cohésion sociale et emploi*, Desclée de Brouwer, Paris

Laville J-L. (Ed) (1994) *L'économie solidaire : une perspective internationale*, Desclée de Brouwer, Paris

Laville J-L. & Cattani A. (2006) (Eds) *Dictionnaire de l'autre économie*, Gallimard, Folio Actuel, Paris

Laville J-L. (2007) "L'autre économie donnerait toutes ses chances à la durabilité" in *La revue durable* n°25, Fribourg

Lipietz A. (2001), *Pour le tiers secteur: l'économie sociale et solidaire, pourquoi et comment*, La découverte - La documentation française, Paris

Loughjin J. (2000), "Regional Autonomy and State paradigm shifts" in *Western Europe in Regional and federal studies* vol.10, n°2 pp10-34

Mc Inroy. (2004) "Le partenariat dans la politique britannique de régénération" in *Développement local, partenariat et approche ascendante: où en sommes-nous maintenant?* Jouen M. Ed , Séminaire n°21 - Notre Europe & ECOTEC (www.notre-europe.eu)

Markusen JR. & Venables A. (1999) "FDI as a catalyst for industrial development" in *European economic review*, n°43 pp 335-356

Martin Ph. (1999) "Public policies, regional inequalities and growth" in *Journal of public economics*, n°73 pp 85-105

Martin Ph. (2001) "Politiques publiques et inégalités régionales" in *Comment renforcer la cohésion économique et sociale après 2006 ?* Jouen M. (Ed), Notre Europe (www.notre-europe.eu)

Morgan B. (2001) "Intégration économique et croissance régionale" in *Comment renforcer la cohésion économique et sociale après 2006 ?* Jouen M. (Ed), Notre Europe (www.notre-europe.eu)

Mothé D. (2006) "La grande démocratie et la petite démocratie" in *Revue Esprit* n°6

Mouhoud El M. (2006)"Mobilité des ménages versus mobilité des entreprises: de nouvelles marges de manœuvre pour l'action stratégique de l'Etat en direction des régions" in *Horizons stratégiques* n°1 Centre d'analyse stratégique

NORDREGIO, (2007) UMS RIATE, RRG Planning & Geoinformation, Eurofutures Finland & LIG, *Regional disparities and cohesion: what strategies for the future*, Study for the European Parliament, IP/B/REGI/IC/2006-201

Pavlinek P. (2004) "regional development implications of FDI in central Europe" in *European urban and regional studies* , n°11, pp47-70

Perrat T J. & Zimmermann J-B. (2003) "Stratégies des firmes et dynamiques territoriales" in Buremeister A et Dupuy C *Entreprises et territoires: les nouveaux enjeux de la proximité,* La documentation française pp15-32

Porter, M. (1998) "Clusters and the new economics of competition" in *Harvard Business review*, Nov-Dec

Putnam R. (1993) *Making democracy work*, Princeton university Press

Ridoux N. (2006) *La décroissance pour tous*, Editions Parangon

Riou St. (2003) "Intégration et politiques régionales en Europe: les enseignements de la synthèse économique géographique-croissance endogène" in *Revue française d'économie*

Robin J. (1989) *Changer d'ère*, Paris, Editions du Seuil

Rodrik D. (1997), *Has globalization gone too far ?*, Institute for international economics Washington D.C .

Sabel Ch. (1996) *Irlande - Partenariats locaux et innovation sociale*, Publications OCDE Développement territorial

Sauvage P. (ed) (1996), *Réconcilier l'économique et le social - Vers une économie plurielle,* Publications OCDE Développement territorial

Stiglitz J. (1998) "Towards a new paradigm for development: strategies, policies and process"

Stiglitz J. (2003) *La grande désillusion*, Livre de Poche, Paris

UNCTAD / CNUCED Geneva (1998) in *The rebel within* Ha-Joon CHANG ed. London, Wimbledon Publishing company

UNCTAD / CNUCED (2006) *Trade and Development Report 2006*, United Nations, New York and Geneva

UNCTAD / CNUCED (2007) *Trade and Development Report 2007*, United Nations, New York and Geneva

Veltz P. (1996) *Mondialisation, villes et territoires*, Presses universitaires de France

Veltz P. (2002) *Des lieux et des liens – le territoire à l'heure de la mondialisation*, Editions de l'Aube, Paris

Venables A. (2005) "Economic geography: spatial interactions in the world economy" in *Oxford Handbook of political economy* Jan

Viard J. (1994) *La société d'archipel ou les territoires du village global*, Editions de l'Aube, Paris

Andreas Weida

The Lisbon Strategy after its 2005 re-launch - Difficulties for regional economic concepts

1. Introduction

The Lisbon Strategy was meant to be a long-term project in many respects. Initiated in 2000 to make the European Union the most competitive economic area worldwide, it has been the subject of analysis and criticism, hopes and deception. Not the least it has revitalised the interest in debates about the correct macroeconomic model for the EU. While 2000 was a year of economic upturn, the widespread feeling that a policy shift was needed in order to catch up in particular with the USA, made it easy for politicians to agree on wide objectives and ambitions. Five years later, in an enlarged European Union and with still more promising growth prospects in the United States, it had to be stated that the expectations in terms of productivity growth as a key to "catch-up" had not materialised. When the European Council endorsed the re-launch of the Lisbon Strategy in March 2005, one of its central features was the focus on its economic pillar, which in itself has been subdivided in three parts. While this has been done mainly for analytical reasons and in order to better structure the National Reform Programmes (NRPs) that have to be presented by all Member States, it was probably also meant to give guidance with regard to the areas of action in which the European institutions see the greatest chance to fulfil the Lisbon goals and to make the EU the most competitive and dynamic economic area with sufficient growth and a marked improvement in employment figures.

This notwithstanding, the division into "Macroeconomic Policy", "Microeconomic Policy" and "Employment Policy" would qualify as a rather peculiar and at least debatable categorization from a theoretical standpoint, as if employment policy would in itself not be clearly interlinked with the social pillar of the overall strategy or if the success of microeconomic measures would not be dependent on a favourable macroeconomic climate. And when the Commission describes possible ways to improve the macroeconomic performance, important factors are actually left out of the "Lisbon thinking".

We will therefore first sum up the basic convictions and possible shortcomings of the Lisbon Strategy before dealing with the criticism that the regional factor has been dealt with insufficiently in the whole process.

2. Theoretical basis for Lisbon's "agreed reforms"

The Lisbon Strategy is on agreeing on objectives and the necessity to implement reforms, but even if the basic direction might be "agreed", the intensity and the instruments are to a large extent left to Member States. Especially with the re-launch of Lisbon Strategy in 2005 the objectives were left untouched, but reporting obligations were simplified and greater instrumental *flexibility* was given to Member States. The Commission thus had learned that this was the only way to avoid having Lisbon classified as an early failure.[1] The three pillar approach has enlarged the criteria according to which economic, environmental and employment success should be evaluated. Within the Integrated Guidelines of 2005[2], the Lisbon economic approach stays however on a mixture of standard supply-side and radical-liberal concepts[3], while keeping also some safeguards for the purpose of efficient market intervention and the correction of market failures.

If one is searching for real new theoretical elements in a unified concept, the assessment of Lisbon - be that before or after the re-launch - gives reasons for severe concern. Instead of a sober analysis of pros and cons of different measures, some basic economic beliefs are repeated and apparent mismatch of objectives and tools[4] is masked by blaming others for an alleged "lack of implementation". In this manner, the "agreed reforms" tend to follow a dogmatic approach without admitting a substantive reality check, which would be useful especially along the timeline of individual Member States macroeconomic hard facts. It is obvious that a benchmarking between Member States does not serve this purpose because it would classify the Member States with a crude beggar-my-neighbour policy as particularly successful. Furthermore only an analysis "over time" would leave scope to criticise the European legal framework and the changes applied to it.

---

1 A thorough analysis of the shortcomings and inconsistencies in the Lisbon indicators up to 2005 is given by Creel, J.; Laurent, E.; Le Cacheux, J. (2005): Delegation in Inconsistency - The Lisbon Strategy record as an Institutional Failure; OFCE Working Paper 7/2005; Paris.

2 The Integrated Guidelines for Growth and Jobs are the result of merging the Broad Economic Policy Guidelines and the Employment Guidelines into one single document. This merging procedure indeed simplified the governance cycle and should not be undervalued. However, it is obvious that no fundamental shift in the theoretical underpinnings of the economic suggestions was intended by going from BEPG to IGs. See Hein, E.; Niechoy, T. (2005).

3 On the theoretical *incompatibility* of neo-classical and radical liberal beliefs see for example Sapir, J. (2006): Theologen der Marktwirtschaft, German edition of "Le Monde diplomatique"; 15.9.2006, orig: "La concurrence: un mythe".

4 On the inconsistency of indicators see Creel, J.; Laurent, E.; Le Cacheux, J. (2005).

One central notion of the Lisbon thinking is "*adaptability*." The adaptability of all actors (state, social security, labour force) to a market-biased solution takes a central role and implies that the theoretical mix is gradually moving towards the radical-liberal side[5]. The same can be said for the modelling of the technology factor and the interpretation of endogenous growth. While the explanation of technology creation through real factors would leave sufficient scope for a deepened analysis of technology-supporting measures, some supporters of the Lisbon growth model start and end from the basic conviction that regulation itself hampers the creation of technology and thus the major growth factor.[6]

One second element is the *individualistic* approach of Lisbon. This is rooted in the partial market approach (financial, labour, goods market) which can in this view each be optimised separately. It also is reflected in the way mutual learning from more successful economies at the same point of time is understood, which means neither learning over time nor assessing one's own country performance vis-à-vis situations in which other policy concepts were implemented.

A third feature of Lisbon especially relevant for analysing the relationship to regional policy is the lack of analysis of *spill-over effects*, founded in the belief that with efficient markets in a stable macroeconomic environment, efficient government intervention could always benefit the active state without

---

5 In radical-liberal schools, economic results are not assessed vis-à-vis macroeconomic parameters like growth or economic development. The best economic results are postulated when the institutional framework is actually approaching an ideal open market solution to be achieved after having defined the property rights of all actors. In this view, further state intervention can never deliver superior results, as it would go against or interfere with the decisions of free individual market participants. The assessment is thus "a-priori".

6 The endogenous growth theory starts from the presumption that marginal productivity of the production factors is not decreasing, thereby building on earlier useful work in production theory. A central feature of more recent models is the expansion of production-oriented services seen as a key factor for technological progress and thus growth. e.g. Guerreri, P: Maggi, B. et al. (2005): Technology Diffusion, Services and Endogenous Growth in Europe, International Monetary Fund Working Paper 05/103. If regulation is there only modelled as hampering the expansion of services and thus technological progress, the Lisbon Strategy is certainly on the right track, as it prescribes further liberalisation. Again, the endogenous growth theory accords growth to the beneficial effect of one central factor, but can neither "explain" why this particular factor should be the central one, nor which policy measures are conducive for the beneficial effect. Zattler, J. (1998): Endogene Wachstumstheorie und wirtschaftspolitische Implikationen für Entwicklungsländer, Discussion paper in Development Economics Nr. 27 ; Justus-Liebig-Universität Giessen; p. 11-12. Models analysing the total productivity effects, thereby leaving scope for modelling increasing, constant and decreasing marginal productivity of single production factors should therefore lead to more insights in the growth process.

harming a neighbour. When negative spill-overs occur, they are either automatically classified as resulting from inefficient intervention (e.g. too heavy subsidies) or sheer neglected (e.g. tax competition). The basic thinking is that a truly internal market would provide a framework dealing avoiding such distortions and that temporary spill-overs only prove a lack of economic integration and not fundamental flaws in the way market equilibria are defined.

This theoretical background is not just a playing-field for economists from different origins. On an important political level, the "success or failure" of Lisbon or more exactly the attribution of the success or failure to different actors (Commission, Member States, social partners) can only be analysed after one has acknowledged that there is some degree of *inconsistency* in the approach itself. Whether a certain policy measures is adequate and might trigger the desired success, depends on the assessment which parts of this theoretical mixture should take priority. Indeed, if one starts from the battle of different theoretical concepts and their subsequent assignment of "adequate policy measures", a lack of implementation of *some* of the Lisbon elements might turn out to be a rather *consistent* Member State approach.[7] Only after that assessment one can decide which Member State "has done best", taking then also into account positive or negative spill-over effects into other Member States. To run a compromise concept with - maybe politically unavoidable - inconsistencies and then putting the blame on Member States for lack of implementation would be a too easy way out.

This idea of "one size does not fit all" should thus be kept in mind. It can turn out that some Member States economies have grown stronger because they have implemented the agreed reforms or rather because they have refrained from certain parts of the Lisbon convictions. The same is true in case of slow growth in Member States, it might be that this results from hastily implementing inconsistent Lisbon-type reforms[8] or it results from failing to implement some of the policy prescriptions. Under the re-launched Lisbon Strategy the most intelligent design of Member States policy would be to implement only the "consistent parts" and thus subscribing to a certain theoretical concept of *growth creation*. A consistent theoretical concept from which policy-makers can derive their measures at least should take into account

7 This is especially valid if one considers the inconsistency of some of the Lisbon operational objectives. The higher employment of women and older workers has been paralleled by worsening situation of other groups. Trying to achieve productivity gains and higher employment at the same time has not been reached by most Member States, because this would have required major technological and training efforts. These however were ruled out from the start by stressing fiscal consolidation and keeping national tax autonomy. Creel, J.; Laurent, E.; Le Cacheux, J. (2005), p. 9 and p.13.

8 Germany's growth performance between 1998 and 2005 is illustrative in this regard.

- the *potential of their economy* (endowment of production factors, role of technological trajectories),
- the *size of the economy* (either a "small open economy" or a large economy, which has to model strategic reaction functions by actors inside and outside the own country)
- and certainly the *priorities of their population* (acceptance of only balanced or unbalanced growth; unequal or equal income distribution; degree of risk aversion and tolerance of volatility in central economic parameters; etc).

To sum up the problem of the theoretical mixture in the Lisbon Strategy and the Integrated Guidelines, one can categorize as follows:
The *standard neo-classical* framework, in principle able for undergoing an empirical test on the success of the policy measures, is inherent in the following convictions:[9]

- the central role of a non-inflationary, stable macroeconomic framework, with the role of the ECB as guaranteeing price stability and supporting other economic policy only in a complementary way;
- the positive role of investment in R&D, to be carried out in the responsibility of private enterprises, however supported by targeted government interventions;
- the support for open *product* markets worldwide, but preferably built on reciprocity in a multilateral legal framework and taking into account market imperfections or distortions;[10]
- the acceptance of the principle of collective bargaining between social partners, however with the target of better taking into account "workplace productivity";
- the idea of wage restraint as being able to combat unemployment, based on General Equilibrium Theory (GET) with a substitutional production function; this is close to a symmetrical explanation of rising and falling unemployment.[11]

---

9 See also Hein, E.; Niechoj, T. (2005); p.12ff.

10 It is remarkable that regarding worldwide *capital* markets the analysis is either more on the radical-liberal side or else the Commission sees the regulation of capital flows as outside EU's competence in a "globally determined" environment.

11 In this regard, normal neo-classical models with their central role of the real wage rate are sufficient to obtain a conclusion in favour of deregulation. However those neo-classical models that model the demand side could still foresee expansive state activity with beneficial growth effects under certain assumptions. To the different models on the European labour market see Hein, E.; Vogel, L. (2007): Distribution and growth reconsidered - empirical results for Austria, France, Germany, the Netherlands, the UK and the USA; IMK Working Paper 3/2007, Düsseldorf, p.1-4. www.imk-boeckler.de.

A slight influence of *neo-keynesian and environmental* economics, matching best with the market failure approach and with only a moderate focus on "technological expenditure" could be derived from:

- the acceptance of the notion to correct market failure in an effective way and with the most efficient instrument, this concept based on standard GET is now the unified legitimation of state intervention after the re-launch of Lisbon; however, it even goes beyond standard practice, insofar as it extends possible interventions on allocative grounds;
- the mentioning of social cohesion as an objective in its own right;
- the acceptance of the environmental pillar as having repercussions on the macroeconomic situation ("positive role of green products and emerging markets in this regard");
- the positive role of state investment in education and research, in certain key technologies beyond a role of only correcting private market decisions.

Radical-liberalism, rooted in the superiority of market solutions (ex-ante) without the need to analyse within a general equilibrium framework and largely immunised against empirical testing of its success, is predominantly visible in:

- the principle of inherent stability of the private sector and the overall support for deregulation "as such", this is matched by the absence of active stabilisation policy through the ECB or the Commission budget;
- the call for reform of labour markets (which includes conviction on the ineffectiveness of demand side measures to combat unemployment - i.e. the NAIRU approach); [12]
- the notion of adaptability of the workforce, including wage differentiation at the workplace (individualistic "market concept" instead of industrial relations with sectoral productivity as the yardstick);
- the call for "fiscal discipline" without analysing positive effects of government demand ("ineffectiveness of fiscal policy in the long run", ultra-rational expectations of market participants), this is matched with the idea of balancing out the budget without analysing the business cycle situation ("unconditional consolidation")[13]

---

12 For a radical-liberal argument it is not necessary to model the development in real wages in order to obtain a conclusion against labour market regulation.

13 It can be argued that theoretical negligence regarding the business cycle was a major problem of the "timing" of Lisbon in 2000. Creel, J.; Laurent, E.; Le Cacheux, J. (2005); p.3. Mabbett, D.; Schelkle, W. (2007): Bringing Macroeconomics Back into the Political Economy of Reform: the Lisbon Agenda and the fiscal philosophy of EMU, in: JCMS 2007, No. 1; pp. 81-103, examine the impact of Lisbon

- the reference to private economic actors along the lines of *formal* equity largely ignoring different starting-positions for the question of optimal organisation of markets;
- the reference to the allegedly dramatic demographic changes (i.e. the understatement of the growth objective and the ensuing redistributive capacity of a growing economy; lack of meaningful distribution measures). The Commission's way to model "demographics" and challenges for pension systems fails to model net wealth effects (including for past decades !) and does not show the actual distributive positions of age cohorts, but it supports the idea that constant *nominal* tax and social insurance contribution rates (!) are the absolute essential of sustainable policy[14];
- the unconditional positive view on the worldwide liberalisation of capital flows;[15]
- the failure to analyse international company mergers as a challenge to the underlying global "market model".

We will now try to shed light on the question whether this mixture of theoretic elements still leaves scope for *regional policy* concepts or if it they are hampered by the Lisbon architecture to such a degree that regions might not longer be able to follow their own path to stronger economic growth within this framework.

3. Regional economic policy concepts in practice

3.1 Theoretical foundations

Regional economic theories have since long evolved along the characteristics of either equilibrium concepts or disequilibrium concepts.

Equilibrium concepts subscribe to the view that an optimal production landscape can be achieved by market forces alone. The market mechanism will

---

microeconomic reforms on automatic stabilizers and find that Lisbon-type reforms weaken the potential for automatic stabilisers within the tax-benefit systems, *without* providing a net gain in terms of largely improved microeconomic efficiency, especially p.98.

14 For a critique on some cohort models see also Rothgang , H. (2007): Unterschiedliche Gestaltungs- und Finanzierungskonzepte der Pflegeversicherung, Hans-Böckler-Foundation; Düsseldorf, p. 24-26.

15 After the establishment of the Currency Union, most neo-classical analysts had expected the EU to engage strongly in efforts to co-ordinate macroeconomic policy globally with major partners. One has to admit that it is difficult to decide whether the relative inactivity in this regard was more because of strategic infeasibility or more because of the Commission taking a different theoretical viewpoint.

respond to the relative scarcity of capital and labour and thus lead to a re-distribution of factors (through migration of capital and labour) as long as marginal productivity is different. A stable equilibrium with optimal production is achieved if all marginal productivities are equal. The task of regional policy would first be to guarantee framework conditions for market mechanisms. These concepts are basically a regional application of General Equilibrium Theory. When in reality regional policy would depart from this theory, for example through large subsidies from the Structural Funds, this would not be legitimated through allocative objectives (growth-inducing policy) but because of mere social redistribution objectives which are - in the first stage - unconnected to the economically optimal market result.

From a methodological viewpoint, disequilibrium concepts can be differentiated into neo-classical and non-neoclassical. The first group explains disequilibria through the normal work of imperfect market forces (central places, polarisation theory, certain agglomeration theories); a correction by policy measures is in principle possible and can try to follow an "optimization" approach. A strong feature of these concepts is that they can explain the emergence of functional regional networks starting from minimal differences in original endowment with production factors including human capital. (f. ex. clusters, economies-of-scale within the production function, input/output optimisation). The second group can either concentrate on individual regions or on regional networks, the focus is on certain important productions factors that gain or lose importance over time, but which can also be influenced through policy measures. These measures are however suggested without the notion of "correcting" markets in order to re-establish an equilibrium, instead the measures should keep the development process running and maintain several options open (e.g. knowledge base approaches [16], certain agglomeration theories,

16 See for example Nelson, R. (1993): National systems of innovation. A comparative study; Cambridge (Mass.) and in empirical terms Paci, R.; Usai, S. (1998): Technological enclaves and industrial districts -An analysis of the regional distribution of innovative activity in Europe; European Regional Science Organisation; Paper No. 461; www.ersa.org. It is remarkable to what extent *some* "modern" knowledge base approaches reduce the idea of networking between different specialised regions and their contribution to overall growth in favour of focusing only on the competitiveness of the *individual region* and the factors (e.g. technology-based innovation, entrepreneurship) conducive to it. e.g. Brioschi, M.S.; Cassia, L.; Colombelli, A. (2005): Common Frameworks for regional competitiveness - Insights from a number of local knowledge economies; paper for the 45th Congress of the ERSA; Amsterdam; p.1-6. The macroeconomic environment of market fundamentalism and scepticism to state planning is thus increasingly reflected also in regional theory. An analysis of *when and why* "knowledge based" competitive regions have really lead to growth creation and not just growth diversion from other regions is largely left out of these "modern" concepts. By contrast, the more traditional disequilibrium concepts (incl.

international product cycle, regional adaptations of "Schumpeterian" approaches). This open dynamics dependant on certain key factors is a common denominator for such modern disequilibrium models.

Over time "cluster concepts" have evolved into one of the main concepts, stemming from the fact that regional economical analysis has proved helpful for gaining insight both in private market forces and public measures that are advantageous for the development of functional networks. This feature of functionality is not confined to maximal regional growth or technical progress but can include stabilisation objectives (resilience against external shocks) and a high degree of content felt by the regional population (e.g. life quality factors beyond growth and unemployment figures). Clusters are in principle able to subsume also some of the non-neoclassical aspects such as knowledge base development and conduciveness to a regional innovation process, however they still are neoclassical in the sense that an "optimal" structure can in principle be deducted and that the *decline* of a cluster would be attributed to an emergence of *dysfunctional* factors (e.g. loss of export markets, technological trajectory, negligence of recreating human capital skills etc.) and not as a proof that development processes are unpredictable and in themselves beyond political steering. In this regard "modern competitive clusters" can even be understood as the attempt to reconcile - at the regional level - individualistic competitiveness approaches and the idea of functional division and specialisation, quite often based on a sectoral input/output analysis.

In order to make cluster concepts more applicable on the policy level, the macroeconomic environment and the either neo-classical, keynesian or radical-liberal set-up of certain framework policies should be included in the model. In this regard, special attention would be made to the

- accepted degree of intervention (esp. room for regulating companies with regard to relocalisation policy, investment incentives, business cycle adjustments),
- supply-side or demand-side preferences (does the concept allow reaction to a "given" demand, does it try to create special markets and consumer orientation or is it predominantly open to support entrepreneurial ideas which search themselves for a market)
- idea whether the behaviour of regions is just mirroring the behaviour of national economies exposed to globalisation (rivalry, delocalisation, tax race) or rather a different, specific *territorial* concept within a market environment.

---

industrial districts) have always taken into account the functionality of a "system of specialised regions" for the objective of overall (national) growth.

3.2. Regional aspects of the Lisbon Strategy

There are several ways on how to analyse especially the regional aspects of the Lisbon Strategy. The definition of the Lisbon Strategy and the process that led to the agreed objectives have been analysed in the literature in some detail. Also the link to the regional policy of the EU and its major instrumental stronghold - the Structural funds - has of course been topical in several contributions, not least in publications by the Commission itself. Thirdly, implementation issues come to the forefront as regional actors are often involved in streamlining existing programmes to the Lisbon objectives. However, also the basic economic foundations of the Lisbon Strategy, its three pillars and the special way in which economic convictions are phrased, can be analysed with a special regional focus. Without trying to summarize the rich existing debate, let us first very briefly refer to the first three items and then concentrate on the fourth.

Concerning the set-up and objectives of Lisbon, there is a wide perception that both the participation of regional actors and the regional impact assessment has been insufficient.[17] Even when at first sight this seems to be somehow unavoidable for a macroeconomic strategy trying to bring Member States as central actors on board, one has to notice that both in 2000 and especially with the re-launch of Lisbon in 2005 two chances for bringing the regional aspect in have been largely missed. The Integrated Guidelines deal with Member States competencies in an overall fashion, which is "striking since many of the policy areas involved (such as employment, social policy, public health and education) are precisely spheres of regional competence in many countries."[18] Furthermore regarding the growth potential and the way to implement certain policy measures with least frictions, regional policy-makers would have possessed the necessary experience to avoid abstract top-down approaches.

Regarding the link from the Lisbon Strategy to actual EU regional policy, the analysis is rather clear-cut and hardly disputed. The Structural funds and the Lisbon Strategy indeed share important goals at the instrumental level. As regional policy traditionally focuses on objectives of growth, stabilisation and distribution, it should already in its current form contribute to tapping the growth potential via investment, including in human capital, infrastructure and innovative productive capacities.[19] In this regard, its instruments are obviously

17 See Committee of the Regions (2005): Implementation of Regions and Cities in preparing Lisbon National Reform Programmes, Brussels, September 2005

18 Heichlinger, A.; Määttä, S.; Unfried, M. (2005): Mid-term Review of the Lisbon Strategy: Regional and Local Players Need to Step Up their Involvement; in: European Institute for Public Administration "EIPASCOPE" 2/2005; p. 47-52, here p.47.

19 Hübner, D. (2005): Regional policy and the Lisbon agenda - Challenges and opportunities, Speech by Danuta Hübner, Member of the Commission responsible for Regional Policy at the London School of Economics; p.2.

in harmony to the Lisbon objectives and the way growth should be triggered allows a stimulating role for the state intervention.[20] However, when referring to "demographic changes" and "globalisation" as reasons for the necessity of economic reforms, not only the analysis of the Commission concerning Lisbon turns radical-liberal with regard to explaining the growth-inducing prospects of such reforms, but also at the instrumental scale the idea of being responsive to the existing regional potential seems to fall victim here. In the end one has to state that the objective to use the long-run growth potential of regions and to create beneficial spillovers, [21] cannot easily be reconciled with the objective to "improve competitiveness across the regions"[22], especially when instead of tapping unused potential in both capital and labour, the adaptability of the population to "labour market developments" is attributed a centre place.

The largest body of analysis concerns the implementation of Lisbon, where also shortcomings and incoherencies are often a reason to complain. Even when regional networks exist and promising concepts like modern clusters or the more recent "knowledge-base creation" have been implemented at regional level, these strategies have been either existed without any link to Lisbon or are merely added-on to it, while innovative concepts on integrating existing schemes under a conceptual "Lisbon roof" are difficult to set up.[23]

Also for this reason it is promising to have one deeper look at the roots of the basic disregard for the regional factor within Lisbon, even after the re-launch of 2005.

3.3. "Delivering on Lisbon reforms" and "encouraging active regions" - two conflicting ideas

The discontent with the way regions and cities have been asked to participate in the Lisbon Strategy is widespread. Even after the *re-launch* of 2005, this

---

20 One should however already point out that the decision which expenditure is growth-oriented and which is not, is not left to Member States, i.e. different economic concepts. The agreed reform path of the Lisbon Strategy permanently seems to imply that support for unemployed or pensioners is detrimental to growth as such, a conviction that is at least radical "supply-side" and would rather merit further analysis. The Lisbon Strategy also falls short of analysing which growth effect can be expected to occur in Europe under current reform policies against the background of globalised capital markets. The notion that public *and* private expenditure (including for pensioners) will trigger more growth than the mere possibility to invest by freeing capital flows (both abroad and in Europe) seems to be ruled out ex-ante without any robust parametrical analysis.

21 Hübner, D. (2005), p.4.

22 Idem.

23 See Heichlinger, A. et al.; p.49 with examples of difficulties to "lisbonize" existing regional policy concepts.

subordinate role can however not be explained by accidental overlook. One could of course argue that over-centralization at Member State level with regard to Lisbon implementation is the organisational reason for this state of affairs. When Member State action at the macroeconomic and structural level is required, there is no feeling of urgency to involve regional actors in the definition of a strategy that is meant to spur overall growth and employment for the EU.

But at a deeper level, it is more likely that the Commission wants to re-establish Member States as central actors for the strategy, leaving out both fiscal responsibility at the European level (where only the monetary framework and an asymmetric restrictive Stability and Growth pact is provided) and fiscal flexibility at lower levels, where interference with an agreed macroeconomic belief would not be considered as adequate. Within this distribution of competences "getting its message through" to all lower levels is a priority. Listening to concerns of lower levels or establishing a true participative structure would not be in conformity with a "top-down" approach that in the end Lisbon is all about. The problem with this approach is that rivalry and competitive use of instruments at national or lower levels might first lead to optimisation at the expense of the partners and then ultimately endanger the acquis itself. The Commission is of course alerted to this danger and reiterates again and again that administrative reforms should not lead to a reduction of acquired rights of workers, citizens and consumers. That this rhetoric is full of good intentions should not be put in question, but the set-up of Lisbon Strategy rather invites at least to some intended "beggar-my-neighbour" policies in the name of competitiveness, thereby placing mainly the burden on the labour factor; it furthermore does nothing to take even unintentional negative spill-over effects into account.

Apart from the consistency problem mentioned before, the positive and negative conditions for meaningful coherent *regional* policy concepts can be summarised as follows:

Negative conditions:

- Lack of commitment by monetary policy to support the growth objective; the macroeconomic set-up has no mechanisms against asymmetric shocks in a monetary union, this means in practice that a regional concept including targeted sectoral development runs a high danger to be swept away in a stabilisation crisis and even more in a substantially changed macroeconomic environment.
- Erosion of financing of regional policy through the erosion of the tax base, lack of fight against tax distortions,
- Repeated allusion to external global factors ("globalisation", "demographics") as unavoidable trends to which all nations have to adapt

- if everything is on "adaptation" to unavoidable global trends already for Member States, than a definition of regional economic objectives seems outdated in itself. The alternative would have been to develop first a sound internal concept that can be defended against external shocks; in this context insufficient regard is currently given to tariff policy and a EU position in the WTO negotiations that would help attaining the Lisbon objectives.
- Relatively central place of the so-called "sustainability" of public finances, a concept which is however neither well-defined by the Commission nor well analysed in its consequences.[24]

Positive conditions:
- Underlining the expenditure for research and development as conducive for growth, thus some degree of optimism in the functionality of technological efforts. Normally the regions can here play a decisive role as they are closer to the R&D potential. Furthermore R&D policy expresses the view that growth is not only determined by market forces. Hereby the Lisbon way is well-founded in standard economic theory; however in operational terms every public effort will suffer from the paradox request to consolidate and cut down, but also to spend more. The easy way out just to "reorient" expenditure lacks understanding of legal obligations towards the own citizens, furthermore any reorientation would need an adequate incentive system. Here it is obvious that the 2 % target advocated for the private sector is simply not matched by rest of strategy.
- Central place of policy learning. This "open" concept includes the possibility of increased awareness to the regional factor as such. It at least gives the option that regions could participate more strategically in future adaptations of strategies similar to Lisbon. The strategic re-launch of "Lisbon" in 2005 has already proven that some political key players are indeed willing to learn from past shortcomings;
- Confirming "market failure" as standard intervention argument from General Equilibrium Theory and thus the lowest common denominator for

24 A basic feature of sound long-term public finances should be that the age cohorts acting as net payers to a public tax or insurance system should be the "richer" generations whereas the generations being net receivers in a long-term should be the poorer age cohorts. It is striking that the Lisbon Strategy fails to tackle the basic necessity to check whether current so-called reforms in Member States actually go against this prerequisite. Instead their is a vague allusion to "ageing societies", a fact that can easily be demonstrated, but should be first analysed for its impact on growth, unemployment and future wages before jumping to the conclusions that it is only or even predominantly a problem for public finances. With regard to sound public finances, Lisbon is not even wrong theory badly applied, there seems to be no theory at all, but activism.

state activity. Hereby the Commission has acted meritoriously by opposing tendencies of putting state intervention into untheoretical "pro-competitiveness" and "not necessary for competitiveness" boxes. Regional agglomeration effects justify consequent state intervention for allocative, not only distributive reasons. Regional policy can thus profit from a wide interpretation of theoretical cases of market failure.

- Re-evaluation of the subsidy instrument (including for SMEs and R&D). The regions can now indeed try their best with more flexibility in permitted subsidies, in this regard R&D support for the own region and for networking activities (as far as possible) are not mutually exclusive.

However, the dominance of "competitiveness" is opposed to the creation of growth through an assessment and use of the existing regional potential. With the common understanding of "agreed reforms" that Lisbon wants to create everybody is tempted to strive for being more competitive in a short-term and individualistic approach. Of course state aid control might come in, if a regional government subsidises heavily. But regional *planning* in a framework that makes sure that all other measures are not taken at the expense of other regions does not receive any attention.

Even fundamental shortcomings in the economic thinking can then be attributed to insufficient implementation efforts, be that by Member States, regions or social partners. Consequently, the question on how a modern federal Europe with strong regions can be politically "brought in", has to be left out. Regions as political entities that act in a market environment do not receive any special "territorial" treatment, they are sometimes erroneously regarded as if being enterprises in somehow beneficial competition or sometimes unfortunately treated as if being nations at a world scale, notwithstanding that the EU would have the possibility of a clearer legal framework and furthermore that regions do not dispose of the same political instruments that nations have.

All that remains for their Lisbon role is that of "implementing agents". A more ambitious unified concept, including a stronger obligation to use certain instruments[25] did not seem feasible, as it would have required an agreement on a regional growth model that could be implemented in a functional network.[26] It is unclear how a "flexible" approach after the re-launch of 2005 can be put in practice at regional level. Which "flexibility" is meant or would be tolerated by the Commission within the Lisbon Strategy ? Should the notion be understood

---

25 For example an impact assessment on regional tax cuts or subsidies; an analysis on how measures respond to the existing sectoral potential of regions, etc.

26 This regional model could still be of neoclassical equilibrium or disequilibrium (e.g. Schumpeterian) type. It would only exclude strictly individualistic models of regional growth, exclusively built on factors that have to be attracted and exports that have to be promoted.

as a flexible instrumental approach on how to attract investment and make the own region more competitive (that is flexibility only within individualistic concepts, see below point 4) or does it really mean that "anything goes", that is that Member States that have somehow managed to keep sufficient money available for active regional policy may do so also in functional networks and with a focus on internal markets, innovation and social needs (non-individualistic concepts) ?

To sum up, regional policy in a Lisbon style is squeezed between different aspirations. As a concept it should be conducive to the overall objectives of Lisbon, that is - still dominant - competitiveness and adaptability to markets which should then in turn lead to growth and jobs. On the other hand, one assumes that through some degree of instrumental flexibility, regional policy can in itself contribute to regional development, including efficient intervention and regard to social and environmental factors, as Lisbon still sticks to the three-pillar approach. However, if the regions would not comply with the budget requirements or complain about tax erosion, if they wish to engage themselves in long-term regional planning they run a high risk that their requests are either neglected or regarded as not compatible with the adaptability feature of Lisbon.

With the assignment of an "implementing agent", every regional policy-maker thus must try to keep a rather heroic balance, serving the own political objectives and agenda for regional growth, but also avoiding to be marked as deviating from implementing Lisbon reforms.

4. The future of European regions - Rivalry or networking ?

Even when at the outset the prospects for regional policy to become a cornerstone of economic revitalisation do not seem favourable, one could of course describe which less ambitious concepts of regional economic development would be fully coherent with the Lisbon set-up.

Introducing the idea of *endogenous growth* seems to be promising. Although this turns out to be a rather minimalist approach to regional development at the instrumental scale, at least the regional policy-makers could support the development of private market potential and market factors conducive to growth. This could still be done under the conditions of open markets and under the presumption of lower tax receipts than in the past and especially by promoting the instrument of public-private partnerships. In such a concept, mutual learning could be understood as learning from the best possible "adaptation record" that went together with only modest cuts in social or environmental expenditure. The way for creating such regional growth poles in Europe based on "individualistic concepts" would still be open. It would neither need considerable new amounts of money nor any U-turn in the way Structural funds have worked until the nineties. As good as such a concept that fully accepts the Lisbon prerogatives sounds, it still seems to be naïve regarding the dominance of macroeconomic decisions. The idea not to raise additional money but to reorient public funding towards growth poles or networks of innovative regions is restricted by the set-up of the macroeconomic framework. If Member States face legal obligations to support certain parts of their population, this money is simply not available for re-orientation to allegedly more "investment-type" use.

It thus remains true even for modern concepts with large adaptability features that the *macroeconomic set-up* within which the Lisbon Strategy is meant to work not conducive to a larger role for "knowledge creation" and innovation. With competitiveness more and more understood not as a tool but an ultimate goal in its own right, the unleashing of private markets is not to be analysed regarding its success, but serves already as an undisputed principle. In this regard budget restriction (Stability and Growth Pact); unrestricted competition in direct taxes and possibly new merger waves in the internal market should even be functional in the Lisbon thinking, as they are all instrumental in limiting the role of state intervention. This definitely must have a negative effect on any regional economic concept that give the state are larger co-ordinating role.

In this regard the argument for regional policy is of course the same as the argument on the paradox of the 3 % objective for R&D investment mentioned before. Also the obligation to use 1 % of GDP to research investment and to spur private actors to use another 2 % cannot help the regions to overcome rivalry and to stress the regional technological potentials.

It does not change the strict requirement to cut down state deficits immediately which limits Member States' room for manoeuvre, the lack of a harmonized concept towards income and business taxation still spurs the race towards very low company taxes. Furthermore, the risk of large revaluations of the Euro - stemming from an exaggerated "external competitiveness" orientation - can lead to a neo-mercantilist attitude towards third markets. A positive net fiscal impetus (whether at national or regional scale) is thus difficult to obtain just by presenting a 3 % objective. Private investment into modern technologies is not spurred by deregulated labour markets which prevail as a concept to combat unemployment. Adaptability to labour markets relies on substitutional production functions and the split between some high-productivity jobs and low-productivity, low-wages services necessary to take up the saved labour force.[27] In such an environment, in spite of tremendous efforts by the public purse, the private business naturally will find *easier ways* to increase profits than investing 2 % in R&D according to the Lisbon objectives.

27 An alternative concept would for example propose real new technological trajectories based on an analysis with limitational production functions and including the reduction of working hours paid-off by large productivity gains.

If for example firms are in the end profitable and competitive on global markets without substantial new R&D efforts and if partial markets seem to run smoothly[28], the Lisbon Strategy has proven to be at least an inconsistent menu. One can thus conclude that the diagnosis that it is necessary to catch-up with the productivity growth of other world regions was correct, but that the instruments suggested were based on insufficient analysis and based on the conviction of the superiority of those regions that are most adaptive to global trends. But this adaptation spurred by globalisation might have been possible with or without European guidelines, a major shortcoming on how to justify detailed efforts through Structural Funds.

The Lisbon ideas of the Open Method of Coordination and increased mutual learning can thus not compensate for other cardinal decisions.[29] Both instruments practically focus on adopting concepts that have worked in individual Member States and not on concepts that *would* work if others (other Member States, other regions) would stop maximise only their own benefits. In this context, mutual learning is totally un-historical, it masks wrong European strategic decisions that have happened in the past as now unavoidable "new framework conditions" to which every region would have to adapt, it disregards the spill-overs which have arisen as a consequence of individual optimisation approaches and it focuses on efficient implementation of measures without monitoring the adequacy of a certain hierarchy of objectives.[30] If any result of individual behaviour under so-called market conditions gets its Lisbon "blessing", an optimal structure of "prospering regions" in the whole EU - influenced both from market forces and optimised state intervention - is not intended. The result will rather be that regional policy-makers engage in a game of fully-fledged rivalry and growth diversion from other European regions and not in network planning.

If at some stage in the future, modern regional concepts of networking, clusters and knowledge base creation should *actively be supported* by the European *framework setting*, the first priority would thus be to reorient strategic thinking to the *growth* objective vis-à-vis other more instrumental or intermediary targets and without further prerogatives. Competitiveness, adaptability, the degree of redistribution and the optimal size of the public sector would then be regarded as of instrumental value, but not work as a-priori restrictions for any strategy. In such a framework which is more focused on

---

28 This would be the "low unemployment, large openness, but still low productivity"-outcome, a service economy with markedly lower productivity growth than the US.

29 Insofar the author is more sceptical than Heichlinger, A, et al (2005); p.48.

30 The rather crude way in which an un-historical concept like individual optimisation "works" for an integrated Community might be caricatured by saying that "Europe would do better if all Member States would raise R&D expenditure, employment level, innovation output etc. on a level x % higher than EU average."

growth, "catching-up" or "falling behind" of regions will only happen in relative and not in absolute terms; it gives more time to regional actors to build a specialization pattern founded on productivity gains through enhancing innovation, intelligent networking and by maintaining precisely those factors that have made European economies strong in the past.

5. Concluding remarks

It is not by chance that the Lisbon Strategy has created uneasiness at the regional level. Its concept is on market adaptability and isolated solutions for every market, furthermore on comparing Member States with different priorities with the same yardstick instead of comparing them over time. At the opposite side, creating growth at a regional level requires a strategic long-term decision whether to try it in autonomy ("individualistic approach") or rather in a network or cluster approach. As the regions that receive spill-overs from your regional policy are also inside your own country[31], Member States favouring autonomy might face an internal *legitimation problem* which as such does not arise at national level, where the Member States are marked as "good pupils" in Lisbon parameters, even if they have achieved this in disregard of negative spill-overs or even through active beggar-my-neighbour policy. Furthermore, a number of "national" policy parameters are no longer at hand, which makes an optimal concept for an individual region extremely *vulnerable* to external shocks.[32]

If Lisbon continues to attribute the need to implement "agreed reforms" to Member States alone, the regions will continue to be "strategy-takers" only. This does not mean that creating a knowledge base or an interregional network would be impossible for the regions in larger Member States, but it means that a

---

31 Small countries have thus little to fear, as they can more easily implement national policies with some additional regional factors and calculate only their overall growth. Most negative spin-offs will happen outside their borders. Furthermore, as Hein, E. Vogel. L. (2007) have shown, small open economies have a greater propensity to a profit-led growth instead of a wage-led growth, thus being able to treat consumption as a by-product and not as a central growth factor. By this taken, a supply-side Lisbon Strategy designed for individual market actors is almost tailor-made for small open economies. In terms of regional economics, concepts of small open economies in an integrated market can even be understood as the last remaining cornerstones of the application of a rigorous export base theory.

32 In this regard a *stabilisation fund* at EU level, where Member States experiencing large growth in an upswing support those in a difficult business cycle position might also be of help for regional policy. In such a framework regional policy would be used to support the conditions for more productivity and growth, while the stabilisation fund would redistribute parts of the benefits of "competitiveness". Originally the stabilisation fund was discussed in the literature as a substitute for the re-valuation instrument which is no longer available in a currency union.

promising regionalisation of a "top-down" strategy would certainly be easier after deep modifications in the instrumental set-up of the Lisbon approach.

The Lisbon Strategy was not meant to shake the world and the basic economic convictions of European policy-makers. In this regard neo-classical macroeconomics (standard supply-side policy), some influx of radical-liberalism, but also the idea of keeping high employment, welfare and environmental improvements as state policy objectives can be understood as a reasonable, because "cautious", approach. Certainly, for politicians neither 2000 nor 2005 was the time for an open commitment to rule-based interventions.

However, by and large, the Lisbon approach cannot escape a debate on the mixture of neo-classical and radical-liberal elements as being theoretically not reconcilable. If the Commission could accept an interpretation that the new instrumental flexibility from 2005 on means that Member States should produce a consistent approach by picking only some Lisbon elements, it would already be an improvement.

From the viewpoint of maximising growth in the EU, it remains on open question to what extent Member States will consider the impact on the partners when designing their "optimal" politics, be that a more market adaptation or growth creation approach. Normally a bottom-up approach will only be developed after having learnt from past mistakes. In this regard non-cooperative strategies will be attractive in the first round, but lose attractiveness over time. At least some policy-makers will note that overall growth performance suffers and that over time the roles of "winning" countries and regions can be entirely reversed. This alone should be sufficient reason for a deeper analysis of economic indicators *over time* and less so *between* countries and regions that - left by themselves - have limited influence on the European framework conditions.

Literature:

European Commission (2005): Communication to the Spring European Council: Working Together for growth and jobs - a new start for the Lisbon strategy - COM (2005) 24

Committee of the Regions (2005): Implementation of the Lisbon Partnership for Growth and Jobs - The Contribution of Regions and Cities - A survey of the involvement of Regions and Cities in preparing the Lisbon National Reform Programmes; Brussels

European Council (2005): Integrated Guidelines for Growth and Jobs; Brussels

Creel, J.; Laurent, E.; Le Cacheux, J. (2005): Delegation in Inconsistency - The Lisbon strategy record as an Institutional Failure; OFCE Working Paper 7/2005; Paris

Daly, H.; Cobb, J. (1989): For the Common Good-Re-directing the Economy Toward Community, the Environment, and a Sustainable Future; Boston

Georgescu-Roegen, N. (1971): The Entropy Law and the economic process; Cambridge (Mass.)

Guerreri, P: Maggi, B. et al. (2005): Technology Diffusion, Services and Endogenous Growth in Europe, International Monetary Fund Working Paper 05/103

Heichlinger, A.; Määttä, S.; Unfried, M. (2005): Mid-term Review of the Lisbon Strategy: Regional and Local Players Need to Step Up their Involvement; in: European Institute for Public Administration "EIPASCOPE" 2/2005; p. 47-52

Hein, E.; Niechoy, T. (2005): Guidelines for sustained growth in the EU ? The concept and consequences of the Broad Economic Policy Guidelines; IMK-Working Paper 2/2005.

Hein, E.; Vogel, L. (2007): Distribution and growth reconsidered - empirical results for Austria, France, Germany, the Netherlands, the UK and the USA; IMK Working Paper 3/2007, Düsseldorf, p.1-4. www.imk-boeckler.de

Hödl, E.; Weida, A. (1999): Die Wirtschaftspolitik der Europäischen Union - Ansatzpunkte und Alternativen fiskalpolitischer Steuerung; Verlag Peter Lang; Frankfurt u. a

Hübner, D. (2005): Regional policy and the Lisbon agenda - Challenges and opportunities, Speech by Danuta Hübner, Member of the Commission responsible for Regional Policy at the London School of Economics

Jerjen, D. (2003): Erarbeitung von Entscheidungsgrundlagen und strategische Steuerung für die regionale Entwicklung; Hochschule Wallis, Siders.

Mabbett, D.; Schelkle, W. (2007): Bringing Macroeconomics Back into the Political Economy of Reform: the Lisbon Agenda and the fiscal philosophy of EMU, in: JCMS 2007, No. 1; pp. 81-103.

Myrdal, G. (1957): Economic Theory and Underdeveloped regions, London;

Nelson, R. (1993): National systems of innovation. A comparative study; Cambridge (Mass.)

Paci, R.; Usai, S. (1998): Technological enclaves and industrial districts -An analysis of the regional distribution of innovative activity in Europe; European Regional Science Organisation; Paper No. 461; www.ersa.org

Rothgang , H. (2007): Unterschiedliche Gestaltungs- und Finanzierungskonzepte der Pflegeversicherung, Hans-Böckler-Foundation; Düsseldorf

Sapir, J. (2006): Theologen der Marktwirtschaft, German edition of "Le Monde diplomatique"; 15.9.2006, orig: "La concurrence: un mythe"

Scott, A. J. ;Storper, M. (1987): High Technology Industry and Regional Development: A Theoretical Critique and Reconstruction. International Social Science Journal 112: 215-232, May.

Zattler, J. (1998): Endogene Wachstumstheorie und wirtschaftspolitische Implikationen für Entwicklungsländer, Discussion paper in Development Economics Nr. 27 ; Justus-Liebig-Universität Giessen.

Silke Tönshoff

Horizon 2010: Local and regional authorities in the Strategy for Jobs and Growth[1]

1. Introduction

It has been argued all along the discussions of the "old" Lisbon Strategy(2000-2005) that the primary flaws dooming it for failure were the missing commitment and engagement of the Member States, the so-called "ownership" and a lack of involvement of other levels of government, a missing "partnership" between the different levels of government.

This article is based primarily on empirical evidence collected between 2005 and 2007 for the Committee of the Regions on the development and involvement of the sub-national level after the re-launch of the Lisbon Strategy in 2005 and on the analysis of the official planning and reporting documents of the Member States (National Reform Programmes and Implementation Reports).[2]

The article tries to respond to the following research questions:

1. Has there been an application of the multi-level governance principle within the renewed Lisbon Strategy?
2. Did the sub-national level participate to a sufficient degree in the revised Lisbon Strategy?
3. Can one observe progress throughout the first governance cycle 2005-2007 at the different stages and in the official programming and implementation documents?
4. Inhowfar does Cohesion policy support the Lisbon Strategy from a local and regional perspective?

Based on these assessments it provides in conclusions implications for the next governance cycle 2008-2010.[3] The article provides a short theoretical overview

---

1 Acknowledgements: Elements of the article reporting on surveys of the Committee of the Regions are based on reports written by the author in cooperation with other CoR staff; Christoph Hofbeck provided the graphs for this article.

2 See Committee of the Regions (2005a, b).

3 While the original Lisbon Strategy of the year 2000 was aiming boldly at surpassing other economic areas by the year 2010, the revised Lisbon Strategy is functioning in governance cycle which are running until the year 2011 and are as Begg (2007) puts it

on the notions and the development of the concept of the "Open method of Coordination" and "multi-level governance" and is based on cross-national evidence of the years 2005-2006 about the involvement of the sub-national level in the Lisbon governance cycle collected for the Committee of the Regions through the following surveys and analyses:

- Summer 2005: Survey among local and regional authorities and national Lisbon coordinators in the preparatory phase of the Lisbon National Reform Programmes
- December 2005: Analysis of the National Reform Programmes
- Summer 2006: Survey among local and regional authorities in the implementation phase of the revised Lisbon Strategy (Monitoring 2006)
- December 2006: Analysis of the National Lisbon Implementation reports

2. Multi-level governance and the Open method of coordination in the revised Lisbon Strategy

Multi-level governance describes how "supranational, national, regional and local governments are enmeshed in territorially overarching policy networks"[4] The concept has its origins in EU cohesion policy and had been applied afterwards to other policy areas. Cohesion Policy and Structural Funds have for a long time been seen as being "the leading edge" of this principle with a more recent debate on the re-nationalization of this policy.[5]

This concept has to be distinguished from the Open method of Coordination at all levels which had been defined by the Lisbon European

no longer focussed on catching up with the US but – more sensibly- at responding to the challenges of globalisation.

4 Marks (1993) p. 402f. See also Piccinetti (2005) for a differentiation between two types of multi-level governance: One which resembles federalism and can be described by the dispersion of authority as being restricted to a limited number of (non-overlapping) jurisdictional boundaries at a limited number of territorial levels while the second type is of a more complex and fluid nature with innumerable and overlapping jurisdictions which tend to be flexible.

5 See Bachtler (2007) who re-assesses the re-nationalization thesis and concludes after examining the concentration and the programming of Structural Funds from 1988 until 2007 that the role of national governments (relative to the European Commission) in key decisions on the implementation of cohesion policy has been exaggerated in the literature and that important arguments underpinning the 're-nationalization thesis' are flawed.

Council Conclusions in the year 2000.[6] The latter is not only focussing on implementation as a distinctive feature but provides also for mutual learning, closer policy coordination through benchmarking and recommendations. The function of the Open Method of Coordination and its development during the two phases of the Lisbon Strategy is particularly visible in the evolution of the annual progress reports of the European Commission which contains in the second phase country specific recommen-dations.

Agenda-setting within the Lisbon Strategy has developed from a "loose wish list" as Begg (2007) describes it to the partnership principle of the Council conclusions 2005: The failure of the first years of the Lisbon Strategy (Lisbon I) had been attributed to excessive complexity and inadequate processes and to a lack of political commitment of the Member States. Lisbon II therefore set out in spring 2005 to refocus on one hand the priorities and to streamline the governance process through a longer programming period, one set of Integrated Guidelines and a reporting of the Member States through National Reform Programmes.

The Integrated Guidelines[7], published by the European Commission, specify that Member States and the European Community should take every opportunity to involve regional and local governments, social partners and civil society in the implementation of these guidelines, and hence in preparing their national Lisbon action plans called National Reform Programmes (NRPs). The OMC has been a substantial concept in the Lisbon Strategy, the development towards a more structured process can be judged by as being rather "a mode of governance" than a form of OMC [8].

The aim of the improved governance cycle is threefold: "to facilitate the identification of priorities while maintaining the overall balance of the strategy and the synergy between its various components; to improve the implementation of those priorities on the ground by increasing the Member States' involvement; and to streamline the monitoring procedure as to give a clearer picture of national implementation of the strategy."[9] As an implicit trade-off it had been assumed that more political ownership of the Member States would be gained at the expense of a transparent assessment process.[10]

---

6 "7. Implementing this strategy will be achieved by improving the existing processes, introducing a new open method of coordination at all levels, coupled with a stronger guiding and coordinating role for the European Council to ensure more coherent strategic direction and effective monitoring of progress. A meeting of the European Council to be held every spring will define the relevant mandates and ensure that they are followed up. Presidency Conclusions (2000).

7 European Commission, (2005) p. 6.

8 Begg (2007).

9 Council of the European Union, Presidency Conclusions, 22 and 23 March (2005).

10 Pisani-Ferry, J. and Sapir, A. (2006).

The new "Partnership for Growth and Jobs-Strategy" as it had been renamed in March 2005 is entering into a new governance cycle 2008-2010. In preparation of this new phase the functioning of the partnership principle should undergo a thorough analysis. This article provides in the following paragraphs evidence that the "partnership" principle with regard to planning and implementation has worked for the sub-national level only to a limited degree.[11]

3. Involvement of the sub-national level 2005-2007

3.1. The planning phase – the development of the National Reform Programmes

In September 2005 the Committee of the Regions undertook a European-wide survey on the involvement of Regions and Cities in the development of the NRPs. While addressing on one hand the local and regional level the survey compared the responses of the sub-national level on the other hand with the responses of the national coordinators of the Lisbon process.[12]

103 answers from the local and regional level out of the 25 Member States and 16 answers from the national level were received. The following graph provides a summary of the local and regional responses.[13] While there was a very high degree of awareness at sub-national level the satisfaction with the process was very limited as well as the perception of a lack of prioritization and a missing planning of appropriate financing sources.

11 This is contrasted by the European Commission on the functioning of the governance process European Commission (2007).

12 Institutional processes and governance structures differ largely from one Member State to another. The consultation processes during the elaboration of the National Reform Programmes reflect these differences. The survey had to respond methodologically to these differences. For a detailed description of the sample and the survey methodology see Committee of the Regions (2005a) p. 23ff.

13 For a differentiation of the results between the local and the regional level see Committee of the Regions (2005a).

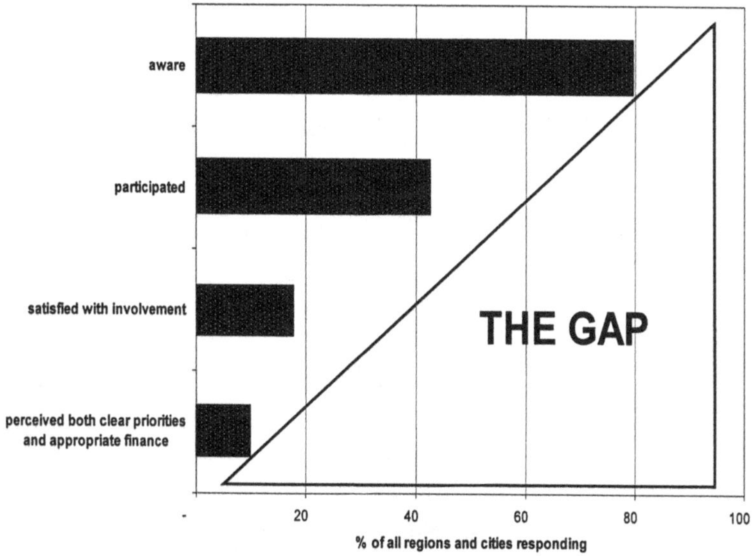

Graph 1: Survey on the involvement in the NRP preparation

Though the participation in 2005 suffered greatly from the short time span between the adoption of the Integrated Guidelines and the deadline for submitting them to the European Commission the following table provides an indication of the differences in perception in the consultation process between the sub-national and the national level.

Table 1 Participation forms in different Member States

Participation form / Member State	Existence of a formal governance process	Meeting of Regions and Cities with the National Coordinators	Regions and Cities participating in the national meeting with the European Commission	Public consultation process	Regions and Cities submitting comments/ proposals
Austria	▒	■	■	□	■
Czech Republic	▒	□	□	□	□
Denmark	▒	■	▒	□	■
Estonia	■	▒	□	▒	■
Finland	□	▒	□	□	■
Germany	▒	■	□	□	■
Hungary	▒	▒	□	▒	▒
Ireland	□	□	□	□	□
Italy	▒	■	■	▒	■
Latvia	▒	▒	□	■	■
Malta	▒	□	▒	▒	▒
Poland	□	□	□	■	■
Portugal	□	□	□	□	▒
Slovakia	▒	■	□	■	■
Slovenia	□	□	□	□	□
Spain	□	■	□	▒	■

■ Yes for all respondents □ No for all respondents ▒ Different perception of the respondents (National Coordinators/Regions & Cities)

The broadest participation was reported for Austria and Italy, where Regions and Cities met both the European Commission and national governments and submitted proposals. In some countries, however, both the NRP National Coordinators and Regions and Cities agreed to report that none of the former happened.

In some Member States, however, (the Czech Republic, Ireland, Portugal and Slovenia), the national, regional and local levels acknowledged that Regions and Cities had not participated. The majority of Regions and Cities stated that they were invited to provide comments on all aspects of the NRP in its preparatory phase. However, when the NRP National Coordinators were asked the same question the response differed. The great majority of respondents answered that they had invited the Regions and Cities to provide comments on all aspects of the NRP in its existing draft. This shows that there are different perceptions between the National Coordinators and the Regions and Cities, with respect to the comments that the latter were invited to provide.

Regarding the uptake of the proposals in the NRPs only 2 out of 10 national coordinators responded that the proposals of the sub-national level would be considered as main contribution while 4 answered that the contributions would be fully taken into account but not seen as main contributions and another 4 stated that the contributions of the regions and cities would be considered either partially or substantially.[14]

3.2. The partnership principle in the National Reform Programmes

When it came to the actual programming documents the NRPs provide a rather mixed picture about the involvement of the sub-national level. The following analysis is solely based on the official documents and the information provided within the documents about the consultation and involvement of the sub-national level. The involvement of the sub-national level is reflected in the degree to which the contributions of Regions and Cities have been taken into account, if the NRPs reflect local and regional approaches and if the NRPs envisage relevant contributions from the Regions and Cities in their implementation. A detailed cross-country analysis is provided in the table at the end of this document distinguishing between the different phases of the governance cycle: Consultation, Implementation and Monitoring.

Though a formal consultation process is rarely reported - a fact which can also be attributed to the tight timetable - several Member States succeeded in organising roundtables, working groups, technical platforms or conferences (AT, EE, FI, DE, IT, LV, MT, NL, PL, SE, SK) and/or ensured consultation in the form of written submissions by Regions and Cities (BE, CZ, EE, ES, HU, UK) during the preparatory phase of the NRPs.

Consultation involving the sub-national level - although depending on the governance structure of the Member State - is reported in less than half of the NRPs (FI, DE, LV, IT, NL, ES, SE, SK, UK, EE). In general, consultation with the social partners seems to have been given greater importance in the NRPs than consultation efforts with Regions and Cities. Information on the consultation process and the involvement of Regions and Cities is rarely provided in the form of a methodological note. Rather, this information is more often either mentioned in a specific paragraph at the beginning of the NRP (NL, EE, PL, SK, DE, AT, SE) or is distributed throughout the programme. Less than

14 Committee of the Regions (2005a), p. 18.

one third of the NRPs do not contain any reference to the involvement of Regions and Cities in the preparation of the NRPs.

The analysis of the NRPs shows that the contributions of Regions and Cities are only presented in a very limited and heterogeneous way. Only a few of the NRPs - UK and Sweden for example - make explicit references to the contributions of Regions and Cities, outlining a clearly recognisable stakeholder input. Likewise, only a few NRPs contain the contributions of Regions and Cities in the annexes of the main text or refer to a specific website where the contributions are displayed (BE, DK, IT, SE, DK).

When the NRP is based on or linked to other strategic planning documents (AT, CZ, FI, HU, MT, PL, SK, SI, ES, UK), consultation in these cases is not only limited to the NRP, but more detailed information on funding and implementation schedules for certain policies is also provided.

The National Reform Programmes have been used by many Member States as stocktaking instruments for reforms that have already started or that have been announced and will continue throughout the governance cycle. Regions and Cities have - depending on the degree of devolution - far-reaching implementation competencies in core areas of the Lisbon Strategy, such as the business environment and better regulation, education and R&D, and innovation policy. Consequently, several Member States acknowledged this systematically in the structure of the NRP and detailed action plans with precise divisions of responsibility between the various governance levels (LT, HU, PL) or detailed divisions for very specific sectoral policy initiatives (AT, BE, CY, FI, FR, ES, LV). Other NRPs foresee an autonomous implementation by the regions, for example Germany, or the development of an implementation plan, such as Malta.

Activities regarding the monitoring of the Lisbon Strategy in the different Member States have been reported in the NRPs only to a very limited degree. They often concern just a few sectoral measures. Only a few countries such as Spain and Greece are following a horizontal approach and establishing independent monitoring agencies. However, regions in some Member States like Italy have specifically requested to be involved in the monitoring phase.

The success of reforms cannot be guaranteed without appropriate financial backing from both the national and the EU budgets. A systematic and horizontal linkage between the implementation and funding of initiatives is provided by a number of countries (CY, MT) while others only mention funding for specific measures (DE, AT, EL, IE, UK, ES).

Being more than a set of political objectives serving to focus discussion and attention in a particular direction, the revised Lisbon agenda would require a subsequent roll-out of budgetary and legislative reforms at different administrative levels. The lack of such a systematic roll-out in form of coherent activities at various levels leads to the conclusion that the role of regions and, to an even larger extent, the role of cities is a limited one.

The CoR undertook a second survey in 2006 (Monitoring 2006)[15] and inquired about the implementation phase of the Lisbon governance cycle: Around 67% of LRAs were either very unsatisfied or fairly unsatisfied with their involvement in the NRP implementation phase of the governance cycle[16]. None were "very satisfied" and only approximately 7% claimed to be "fairly satisfied". The remaining LRAs felt "neutral" towards this question. A few LRAs stated that they were contributing towards the member states' NRP implementation reports[17]. There was also dissatisfaction amongst LRAs with regard to the monitoring stage of the Lisbon governance cycle, with the vast majority claiming to be either very unsatisfied or fairly unsatisfied with their involvement in monitoring the NRP's progress.

3.3. Sectoral priorities in the NRPs – a local and regional perspective

One of the main objectives of the revised Lisbon Agenda was to deliver a clear message on the Union's priorities over the next few years. To achieve these objectives, the Union should "mobilise all the resources at the national and Community levels". Regional and local governments, social partners and civil society should be involved in the implementation of the Integrated Guidelines as stated in the basic strategic document.[18]

According to the results of the survey conducted by the Committee of the Regions on the involvement of the Regions and Cities in preparing the NRPs in 2005, the Regions and Cities and the NRP National Coordinators recognised the setting of clear priorities as the main added value of the NRPs.[19] Some NRPs specified the priorities in a very concise way and link them to the specific guidelines, whilst others approach this issue in a more general way.

The results of the CoR's survey showed that Regions and Cities are mainly interested in the Microeconomic and Employment fields. They are committed to helping improve microeconomic conditions, namely to create an attractive environment for business, promote entrepreneurship and SMEs, Research and Development. Regions and Cities also aim to support the main

15 Committee of the Regions (2006).

16 62% of the participants in the monitoring exercise answered to the question on the level of satisfaction of LRAs with their involvement in the implementation and monitoring stages of the Lisbon governance cycle.

17 These were submitted by Member States to the European Commission on October 15, 2006.

18 European Commission (2005) p.6.

19 See Committee of the Regions (2005a).

employment reforms, particularly in education, training and matching of skills to job offers.
The priorities of Regions and Cities are to a large extent recognised as the main objectives in the NRPs. The following paragraphs analyze the role of regions and cities in the NRPs with regard to the above mentioned key challenges.

In the NRPs, Regions and Cities assume a particular role in the moderation of regional differences of employment, supporting of job mobility, linking of education with employment, improving matching of labour needs. In this respect, a number of initiatives are foreseen by the Member States. In the Czech Republic regional labour offices are set up to allow for a single employment policy across the whole territory. A particular initiative linking education with employment has been foreseen by the Slovak Republic in its NRP: A national programme for learning regions, ensuring the conformity of the regional demand for programmes of further education and the real needs of the job market in the regions.

The linkage of science, research and business is a very important objective in the NRPs. The measures to be taken by some Member States (EE, DE, FI, NL, FR, PL) foresee an involvement of regional and local authorities in stimulating cooperation between authorities, business and knowledge/research institutes. Regions and Cities have according to the NRPs an important role to play in the implementation of reforms concerning the improvement of the business environment. Policy proposals regarding the regulatory environment are put forward by the majority of Member States (CZ, EE, EL, ES, FI, IT, NL, PT, SI, SE, SK, CY, MT). Only some Member States however mention that the sub-national level should improve the investment climate by decreasing regulatory issues to ensure better services for citizens and enterprises (NL, DK).

Table 2: Key challenges as identified by Member States

Key challenges	Identified by	MS
Utilisation of labour	AT, BE, CZ, DK, EE, EL, ES, FI, FR, HU, IE, LT, LU, LV, MT, NL, PL, PT, SE, SI, SK, UK	22
R&D and innovation	AT, BE, CY, CZ, DK, EE, EL, ES, FI, FR, HU, IE, IT, LT, LU, LV, NL, PL, PT, SI, SK, UK	22

Key challenges	Identified by	MS
Business environment (incl. better regulation and Internal Market)	**AT, CY, CZ, DK, EE, EL, ES, FI, FR, HU, IE, IT, LT, LU, LV, MT, PL, PT, SI, SK**	**20**
Education and lifelong learning	**AT, BE, CY, CZ, DK, EE, EL, ES, HU, IE, IT, LV, LT, LU, MT, PL, PT, SI, SK, UK**	**20**
Sustainability and quality of public finances	**AT, BE, CY, CZ, EE, EL, ES, FI, FR, HU, IE, LT, LU, LV, MT, PL, PT, SI, UK**	**19**
Environmental sustainability	**AT, BE, CY, CZ, DK, EE, ES, FI, IE, IT, LU, MT, PT, SI, UK**	**15**
Competition	**CY, DK, EL, ES, FI, HU, IT, LV, PT, SE**	**10**
Infrastructure	**AT, CY, CZ, ES, FI, IE, IT, PL**	**8**
Social cohesion	**BE, CY, FR, IE, PT**	**5**
Public sector improvements	**DK, FI, SI**	**3**

Macroeconomic Microeconomic Employment

Source: Report on Lisbon National Reform Programmes 2005, ECFIN/EPC(2005)REP/55392 final (modification with colours by the Committee of the Regions).

It is recognised in a number of NRPs that the main condition for boosting entrepreneurship is the reduction of the administrative burden at the decentralised level (DE, DK, SI, SK, NL). In this context, many Member States highlight the progress that has been made with the introduction of impact assessments measuring the burden of regulation on businesses on sub-national authorities (CZ, DK, FR, IE, NL, PL, SI, SE, UK). A few Member States also set quantitative targets (SE, NL, DK). Some Member States foresee an audit of barriers to business or impact assessments both on the central and on the local and/or regional level (DE, SK).

The need for sustainability of public finances is recognised by all Member States in their NRPs. Many Member States mention the need to reduce the budget deficit and public debt. In this respect, key reforms are foreseen in public expenditure on health care and pensions. Some Member States stress the role of Regional and Local authorities with regard to public expenditure (DE, ES, CZ, EE, FI, PL, EL). In addition, organisational and structural reforms to ensure a more efficient allocation of financial resources are envisaged or are already ongoing in some Member States (FI, EL, PL).

4. The link between the Lisbon Strategy and Cohesion Policy

4.1. The link between the governance processes

Governance of EU Cohesion Policy is not undisputed: On one hand numerous researchers claim to have observed since 1988 a "re-nationalisation" of design and implementation of the funds allocation and on the other hand the position that the structural funds constitute the "leading edge of a system of multilevel governance" with a system of shared powers among the European, national and regional level. With the reforms in 1988 several principles have been introduced which still remain at the heart of cohesion and structural funds such as concentration (on a limited number of objectives), programming (strategic, multi-annual plans) additionality (avoidance of crowding out of national funding) and partnership (between the European, national and regional level in design and implementation)[20].

There exist various mechanisms for fostering a link between the Lisbon Strategy and Cohesion Policy: Formally, the strategic dimension of Cohesion Policy is strengthened by two new elements: the Community Strategic Guidelines at the European level and the National Strategic Reference Framework (NSRF) at the national level. On the basis of the priorities indicated by the Community Strategic Guidelines, EU Cohesion Policy offers a relevant contribution to main policy challenges at the core of the Lisbon agenda.

The European Commission's Annual Progress Report highlighted in 2006 the need for stronger efforts to develop coordination mechanisms between those responsible for the national reform programmes and those preparing the structural funds programmes, for the period 2007-2013.[21] In this context, the National Strategic Reference Frameworks' strategic process (planning; implementing, monitoring) differs quite substantially from the governance cycle of the NRPs with its long multi-annual planning and financial framework combined with the "partnership principle", which was introduced by a regulation in 1988.

There is a striking divergence between the levels of satisfaction amongst LRAs in the planning process of the NRPS and the NSRFs: In a second survey in 2006 (Monitoring exercise 2006) the Committee of the Regions inquired

20 See Bachtler (2007) for a discussion of the two positions and a longitudinal perspective on concentration (spatial distribution of funding) and programming (thematic allocation of resources).

21 European Commission (2006).

about the specific linkage between the Structural Funds and the Lisbon Strategy from a local and regional perspective.[22]

Approximately 47% of LRAs claimed to be either very satisfied or fairly satisfied with their involvement in the NSRF planning process. However, room for improvement was reported concerning the infra-regional level. The relatively high level of satisfaction with the NSRF process contrasts with a meagre 14% of LRAs claiming to be fairly satisfied with their involvement in the planning process of the NRPs. No LRAs were "very satisfied" with their involvement in the NRP planning process.

It is perhaps unsurprising then that LRAs got more actively involved during the NSRF planning phase than was the case for NRP planning. According to the CoR's survey in 2005, the Regions and Cities found that the draft NRPs present a less cohesive approach than that claimed by the national authorities. Furthermore, only 13% of all respondents stated that the NRPs foresee appropriate financial resources for regional and local development. For the new financing period 2007-2013, the main objectives of the Cohesion Policy are to ensure greater ownership on the ground. This can be achieved by a reinforced dialogue, a clearer and more decentralised sharing of responsibilities and the strengthening of the strategic dimension to ensure that Community priorities are better integrated into national and regional development programmes. These objectives have been taken up in the National Reform Programmes to a widely varying degree.

National Reform Programmes can strongly build upon the planning and budgetary leverage of the Cohesion Policy. Whereas some National Reform Programmes establish a clear link with Cohesion Policy (EL, FI, IE, PL, SE, SI, AT, IT), a stronger link is needed in the majority of the National Reform Programmes. Only a few Member States presented a systematic cross-link analysis between the National Reform Programmes and the provisional drafts of the National Strategic Reference Frameworks (PT, AT, IE, UK, CY). However, some Member States, such as Sweden, expressed their intention to improve this coordination. EU Cohesion Policy has been able to inspire and support relevant governance and managerial innovations within public administrations, an essential success factor of the Lisbon agenda. This "process-related" contribution of Cohesion Policy to economic growth is recognised in a number of NRPs.

---

22 65 local and regional authorities responded to the survey. For a detailed analysis and the sample composition see Committee of the Regions (2006).

Graph 2 Level of satisfaction NRP & NSRF Planning

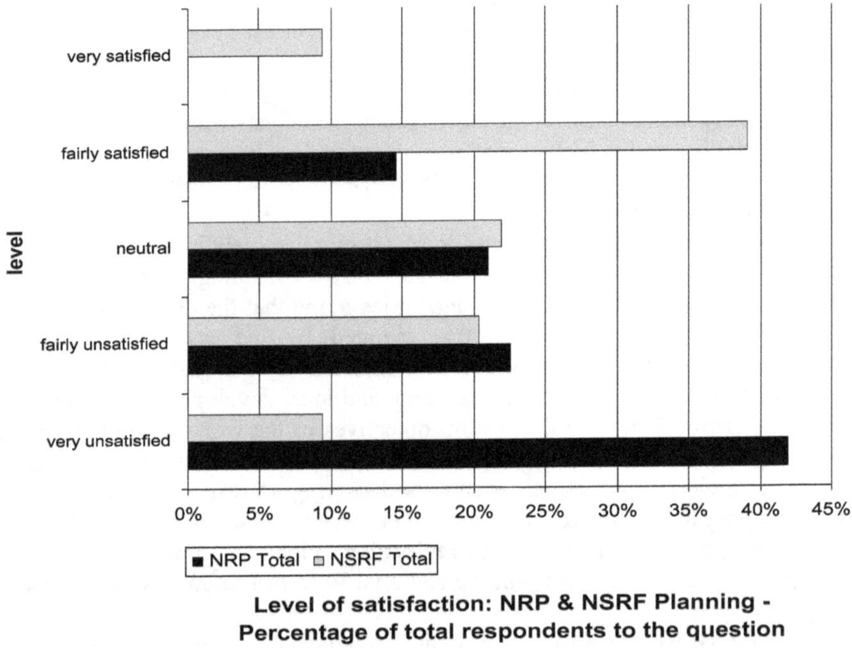

Cohesion Policy can provide a framework for structuring integrated policies on the ground, addressing questions like innovation and entrepreneurship and access to finance as it was indicated in the NRPs of PT, EL, IE, ES. Institutional capacity building is described as necessary to attract and effectively manage financing from the structural funds (LV, EL, SI, CY, EE).

The link between Cohesion Policy and the Lisbon governance process is strengthened from 2007 on when Member States are obliged to report on the contribution of the Cohesion Policy to the realisation of the NRPs' goals.

Graph 3 Degree of involvement NRP and NSRF Planning

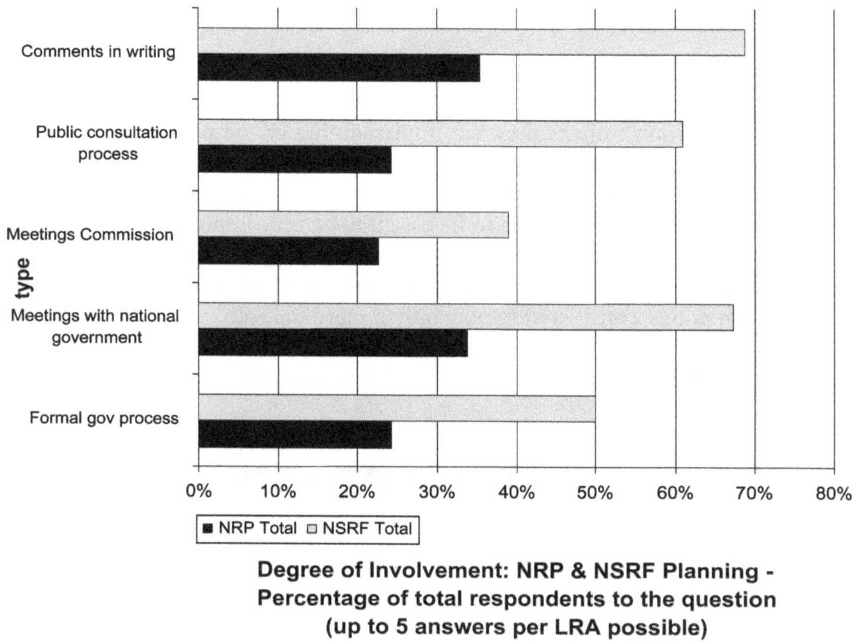

4.2. Funding the Lisbon Strategy on the local and regional level

Respondents to the Monitoring exercise 2006 of the Committee of the Regions were asked to evaluate the contribution of the Cohesion Policy to Lisbon type actions/projects they are implementing or are planning until 2010. Graph 4 below clearly illustrates the great importance that LRAs accord to the cohesion policy. In approximately 60% of all Lisbon actions described by LRAs the cohesion policy is considered to be essential or very important in the funding of these. The infra-regional level deems this to be slightly more important than the regional level. In a relatively small percentage of actions (under 10%) was the cohesion policy considered to play only a marginal role.

Graph 4: Contribution of Cohesion Policy to Lisbon-type actions

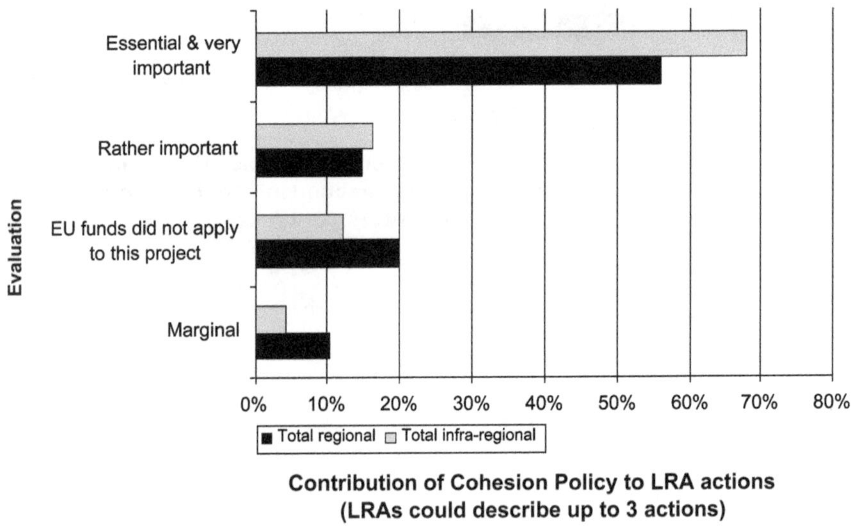

Furthermore, the Cohesion Policy was regarded as essential or very important in a slightly higher percentage of actions from the new Member States in comparison to the EU-15 LRAs.

Graph 5: Relative Importance of funds

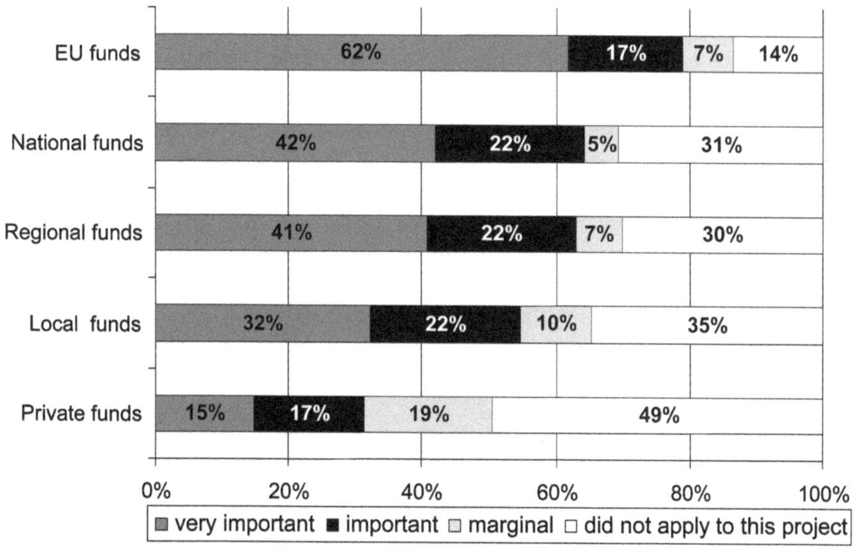

Relative Importance of funds for Lisbon-related Actions (total)

Conclusion

The new form of governance defined as the "partnership for growth and jobs" which is supposed to involve all stakeholders, also local and regional government, has worked only partially for the sub-national level. According to the survey in the planning and programming phase of the strategic documents of the revised Lisbon Strategy there is on one hand a very high degree of awareness among the regions and cities but on the other hand also a very low degree of satisfaction with the process. A survey one year later – with a different sample – led to the same picture about the implementation phase of the revised Strategy.

For being more than a set of political objectives serving to focus discussion and attention in a particular direction, the revised Lisbon agenda would require a subsequent roll-out of budgetary and legislative reforms at different administrative levels. The lack of such a systematic roll-out in form of coherent activities at various levels leads to the conclusion that the role of regions and, to an even larger extent, the role of cities in the governance cycle 2005-2008 is at best a limited one. Regions and Cities are mainly interested in the Microeconomic and Employment fields. They are strongly committed to helping improve microeconomic conditions, namely to create an attractive environment for business, promote entrepreneurship and SMEs, Research and Development. Regions and Cities also aim to support the main employment reforms, particularly in education, training and matching of skills to job offers. The priorities of Regions and Cities are to a large extent recognised as the main objectives in the NRPs.

The various links and dependencies between the Lisbon Strategy and Cohesion Policy are particularly strong for the "process-related" contribution of Cohesion Policy to economic growth and the funding of Lisbon-type activities of the sub-national level. The requirements for the reporting on earmarking from 2007 onwards will potentially strengthen the cross-referencing and also the coherence between Cohesion Policy and the Lisbon Strategy as well as the policy coordination between the different actors involved.

Literature

Bachtler, John F. and Méndez, Carlos (2007): Who Governs EU Cohesion Policy? Deconstructing the Reforms of the Structural Funds; JCMS: Journal of Common Market Studies, Vol. 45, Issue 3, pp. 535-564, September 2007 Available at SSRN: http://ssrn.com/abstract=1007100 or DOI: 10.1111/j.1468-5965.2007.00724.x

Begg, Iain (2007): Lisbon II, Two years on: An Assessment of the Partnership for Growth and Jobs; Special Centre for European Policy Study Report.

Committee of the Regions of the European Union (2005a): Implementation of the Lisbon Partnership for Growth and Jobs – The Contribution of Regions and Cities A survey on the involvement of Regions and Cities in preparing the Lisbon National Reform Programmes.

Committee of the Regions of the European Union (2005b): Regions and Cities in the National Reform Programmes – A test case for the partnership for Growth and Jobs – An analysis of the presentation of the local and regional perspective in the National Reform Programmes.

Committee of the Regions of the European Union (2006): Horizon 2010 – local and regional authorities for Jobs and Growth.

Council of the European Union (2005): Presidency Conclusions 22 and 23 March.

Council of the European Union (2000): Presidency Conclusions 23 and 24 March.

Economic Policy Committee (2005): Report on Lisbon National Reform Programmes; REP/55392 final.

European Commission (2005): Integrated Guidelines for Growth and Jobs (2005-2008); COM (2005) 141 final of April 2005.

European Commission (2006): "Time to Move Up A Gear" - The European Commission's 2006 Annual Progress Report on Growth and Jobs: http://ec.europa.eu/growthandjobs/annual-report_en.htm

European Commission (2007): "Information Paper No. 1: Earmarking"; http://www.oerok.gv.at/EU_Regionalpolitik_in_Oesterreich/strukturfonds_2007_2013/rechts grundlagen/EC-Note1_Earmarking%20_COCOF_07_0012_00_EN-FINAL20070228.pdf.

European Network of Economic Policy Research Institutes (2005): Is the European Economy a Patient and the Union its Doctor? On Jobs and Growth in Europe.

Marks, Gary (1993): Structural Policy and Multi-Level Governance in the EC, in: Cafruny, A. and Rosenthal, G (eds.), The State of the European Community: The Maastricht Debate and Beyond; p. 391-411.

Piccinetti, Leonardo (2005):Europeanization and Britain:Towards Multi-level Governance? Paper presented at the EUSA 9th Biennial Conference in London.

Pisani-Ferry, J.;Sapir, A.(2006): Last Exit to Lisbon; in: Bruegel Policy Contribution; March 2006.

Annex

Country	Consultation Process	Implementation Process	Monitoring Process
Austria	A Reform Dialogue took place in May 2005 with social partners and other stakeholders. Regional Representatives participated in the Reform Dialogue. The Länder participated in meetings preceding strategy panels (e.g. platform Innovation since summer 2004, scientifically accompanied by the Institute for Technology and Regional policy of Joanneum Research).	Information provided for specific policy areas.	No specific details.
Belgium	Intense interaction between the Federal government, Regions and Communities for the preparation of the NRPs. Social partners were also consulted.	Regions and Communities will implement the NRPs' provi-sions in the areas of their competences. The important role of the social partners is also underlined in the Belgian NRP.	No specific details.
Cyprus	Social partners, political parties and the private sector were consulted.	Ministries will be primarily in charge of implementing the NRP. However, the following will also be involved: a research promotion foundation, the institute of technology, the Cyprus productivity centre, a tourism and sports' organisation.	The NRP will be published on the Ministry of Finance's website. All stakeholders will be invited to provide suggestions for an effective monitoring mechanism. A set of indicators will be developed starting with the core structural indicators and bi-annual progress reports.

Czech Republic	Consultation of Economic and Social Partners; Chamber of Deputies; Senate of the Parliament of the Czech Republic.	The central authorities will mainly implement the NRP provisions. However, in the area of employment policy the social and economic partners will play an active role via the Council of Economic and Social Agreement. There are no specific details about the role of regional and local authorities.	No specific details.
Denmark	Annex 8.2.of the NRP includes contribution from social partners on the largest public labour market, namely the municipal and county-municipal sector. Written comments are also inserted in Annex 8.2.	No specific details.	No specific details.
Estonia	A Working Group was established in order to participate in the preparation of the NRP and this involved local government institutions. Then the latter attended the meetings of the Group and/or submitted written proposals. The local authorities could also have made comments during the period of public debate when the NRP was put on the Internet (27 September – 7 October 2005).	The Secretary of State will coordinate the implementation process. The Working Group will play a role in implementing and updating the NRP's regular implementation reports presented by the Secretary of State.	The Secretary of State will coordinate the monitoring process. The Working Group will evaluate the outcome of the process.
Finland	The social partners and the local government were consulted. Two major seminars took place for preparing the NRP. The first one involved representatives of the social partners in the labour market, local government and the science community; and the second one involved representatives	For example, in the field of innovation strategy, processes will be developed that will lead to a more effective coordination of regional and local innovation policy and national innovation policy.	No specific details.

	of independent NGOs. The NRP has also been discussed in the Economic Council and the Committee on Labour Policy, and has been brought to the attention of Parliament.		
France	On the basis of the NRP only social partners were consulted.	Territorial entities will intervene in certain areas such as employment, public services, information society.	
Germany	A group of 4 Länder (2 A and 2 B Länder)[23] represented the Länder in the consultation process with the Bundesregierung and have formulated priorities for the NRP which have been supported by all Länder. German Bundestag, central municipal associations, Business Associations and trade unions have received the report for information. The Bundesrat and the Bundestag were not formally consulted.[24]	The different Länder will autonomously implement the NRP measures in the areas of their competences.	
Greece	Social partners, Regions and NGOs representing Civil Society were consulted in Greece.	The NRP provides few example of involvement of the regional and local authorities for the implementation of NRP measures. For instance, with regard to the sustainability of Public Finances, the government is pursuing many structural reforms, one of which includes	

23 A and B Länder is an informal term describing, respectively, Länder governed by the SPD and Länder governed by the CDU.

24 Germany held federal elections on 18 September 2005. The NRP was therefore drawn up under great time pressure and without wide-ranging consultation.

		improvements in the fiscal auditing system, aiming at increasing efficiency in the allocation of public funds. These include, inter alia, the setting up of internal auditing services in the Ministries, the local authorities and public entities in general.	
Hungary	There was a wide consultation of experts and social and economic partners in Hungary, but regional and local authorities are not mentioned in the NRP.	The Hungarian NRP specifies the bodies responsible for reforms, in specific cases local governments are responsible for implementation of reforms. The instruments for realisation of reforms are also specified. Local authorities are involved mostly in designing and implementing employment programmes and programmes for the integration of minorities or disadvantaged people.	
Ireland	The department of the Taoiseach coordinated the overall preparation of the NRP. An extensive consultation took place with relevant departments and agencies in the preparation of the programme; the social partners; both houses of the Oireachtas (Parliament). An ongoing dialogue was also pursued with the European Commission, as well as bilateral discussions with a number of Member States.	No specific details.	No specific details.
Italy	In Italy, there was an extensive consultation with Social partners. The regional representatives were considered among the	The actors of the Italian NRP implementation will be: the regions, autonomous bodies and the social partners. For	There are no further details in the NRP about a general follow-up. However,

	'social partners'. The 'Social Partners' joined the inter-ministerial NRP taskforce. In addition, the contribution from the Conference of the Presidents of Regions and Autonomous Provinces is attached as an annex to the NRP document.	instance, they will contribute, among other things, to simplifying and improving regulation and to introducing a stable coordination of responsibilities in the field of tourism, improvement of spending capability, especially via the introduction of instruments of vertical cooperation between central and regional government administrations.	there will be, for example, a specific follow-up of local Agenda 21 processes and other pilot measures to increase sensitivity to environmental issues. And in the framework of the Cohesion Policy, a sharing culture of measurement, evaluation and assessment will be set up, including with the help of the newly set up assessment unit network (32 units in central and regional administrations, with the involvement of over 350 experts); as well as instruments of vertical co-operation between central and regional administrations, in particular the 350 Programme Framework Agreements executed between states and regional Authorities.
Latvia	No specific details.	The government has established the	

		Supervisory Board of the Lisbon Strategy, chaired by the Minister of Economics. Ministers and representatives of the Saeima (Parliament), local governments and social partners are included in the Board. The Board will coordinate implementation of the NRP and inform the public about the fulfilment of the tasks. The social dialogue at regional level will be reinforced.	
Lithuania	Social partners; ministries; industry and those SMEs concerned by specific actions, especially with the creation of consultation centres will be consulted. However, there is no specific mention of consultation with regional and local authorities.	The national authorities will be in charge of implementing the NRP measures, as well as the regional and local authorities. A detailed action plan was established specifying authorities/bodies/organs in charge of the execution/realisation of each action. In specific cases, the regional and local authorities are involved together with organs from the central level. The deadlines and the necessary resources for realisation are also indicated.	No specific details.
Luxembourg	Both the executive and legislative branches were consulted in Luxembourg, as well as other public authorities and social partners. In addition to the economic players, the Government will invite "the whole of Luxembourg to participate in the	There is no detailed information on the implementation process and its protagonists. However, references to regional and local authorities in different areas can be found: sustained development (town reforms),	The appendices of the NRP cover the recourse to Competitiveness Indicators, yet there is no further detail about the participation of

	modernisation effort currently underway in the country".	improving Luxembourg connectivity via cross-border/trans-national/interregional cooperation (FEDER), ensuring maximum coordination and integration between sectors with the reform of municipalities (supra municipality cooperation and development of regional plans).	regional and local authorities in the monitoring and evaluation process.
Malta	In Malta, consultation took place with Government stakeholder entities and the social partners via one-to-one meetings. A launch conference was also organised.	Ministries (one of which is the Ministry for the Gozo region) are to be requested to develop specific project plans and will be responsible for the implementation of the measures falling within their portfolio. Social dialogue also plays an important role.	The Management Efficiency Unit will be assigned the role of monitoring and reporting on the implementation progress. Throughout the timeframe of the NRP, regular reporting on the status of achievement will be forthcoming in order to keep all stakeholders well-informed of the achievements registered.
Netherlands	The Dutch NRP includes a separate paragraph explaining the process of preparation of the NRP. It mentions explicitly regional and local authorities, especially that they have a role in the reform agenda for instance in the field of innovation, spatial planning and management of delays. That is why the regional and	No specific details.	No specific details.

	local authorities were involved via regular "consideration platforms".		
Poland	A broad consultation process took place in Poland with civil society. However, regional and local authorities are not explicitly mentioned in the NRP concerning the consultation process.	The NRP indicates, in specific cases, the timeframe and actions to be taken for realisation of reforms for regional/local level.	No specific details.
Portugal	No specific details.	No specific details.	No specific details.
Slovak Republic	The NRP was submitted to an open public discussion before the approval by the government. There was then an active involvement of representatives of almost all areas of Slovak society.	The NRP mentions that regional and local authorities will play specific role in fulfilment of the programme. Annex 1 of the NRP includes proposed objectives and measures to be taken; yet the authorities responsible for it are not mentioned.	No specific details.
Slovenia	Slovenia's Development Strategy (SDS) was adopted by the Government in June 2005, integrating the Lisbon goals within the national setting on the basis of a broad consensus and comprehensive public debate that involved public stakeholders. Several public discussions on the draft SDS were organised with individual organisations (consultations held by the President of the Republic, the Sustainable Development Council, the Economic and Social Council, the Chamber of Crafts, the Chamber of Commerce and Industry, non-governmental and	After having adopted the SDS, the Government established the Committee of Reforms, which is a task force comprising some 150 experts from universities, enterprises and the civil service, and commissioned it to put forth specific measures for implementation of the SDS in the areas of competition, higher economic growth and employment.	

	regional organisations).		
Spain	In Spain, a wide consultation took place during which the following stakeholders were invited to express their priorities: the social partners, chambers of commerce, Parliament, the Autonomous Communities and local corporations.	The Social partners, the Autonomous Communities and Parliament will play an important role in the implementation process. For instance, the new budget stability law will respect the financial autonomy of the Autonomous Communities and seeks to find wide consensus in determining the stability objectives.	Evaluation and monitoring mechanisms will be put in place in which the social partners, chambers of commerce, the Parliament, the Autonomous Communities and local corporations will participate. Moreover, the Spanish Government intends to meet the representatives of the Regions, Parliament, the Chambers of commerce and the rest of the agents that have collaborated in the elaboration of the NRP, at least twice a year.
Sweden	In Sweden, there was consultation with the social partners, civil Society and the regional and local levels.	The NRP specifies that the responsibility for the implementation of regional development policy in Sweden is shared between national and regional levels. Considering the local level, it adds: "A number of Swedish local municipalities have, on a voluntary basis, launched a process to prepare local initiatives for growth and employment in line with	

		the Integrated Guidelines and the Lisbon targets. The Government welcomes these initiatives and regards them as important contributions to a coherent implementation of the Lisbon strategy throughout the country".	
United Kingdom	The UK government generally consults widely with national, regional, local and sectoral stakeholders in developing proposals for structural economic reform. The development of the NRP benefited from the involvement of key stakeholders, many of whom submitted detailed observations and recommendations for economic reform in the UK.	Regarding the promotion of productivity growth, Government policies are implemented at the regional and local level through Regional Development Agencies (RDAs), Regional Assemblies, and local authorities. The devolved administrations in Scotland and Wales, and the Northern Ireland administration, have responsibility for economic development.	

Bernard Chane Kune

Decentralisation, decentralised cooperation and economic development

1. Introduction

Nowadays, almost all countries in the world are facing to a common set of questions or characteristics. For sure intensity, potential consequences and means available to confront them are different from one country to another, but the nature of many issues is in a large extent at least very similar all around the world.

Among the shared phenomenon of the current world is globalisation. It is no more a recent or an unknown phenomenon. While its causes, effects, consequences, forces and weakness are one of the most hotly-debated topics of the last decades, none can ignore the globalisation. It is a fact. Fundamentally, it embraces many dimensions underlying a greater and higher level of relation, integration and interdependence in many fields such as economy, ecology, social or culture. One of the greatest evidence of this globalisation process is probably the urge increase in international trade. During the last fifteen years for example, world trade growth rate has been almost two times more important than the world production increase.

Another and second common dimension in nowadays world is the general trend toward an increase of decentralisation. While this change can be seen as another aspect and/or consequence of the globalisation, it also expresses the incontestable strength and will to take into account specific conditions encountered at regional or local levels. It additionally expresses the need to adapt, when relevant, policies to these conditions. Fundamentally, increasing and deepening decentralisation, meaning transfer of authority and responsibility from central to regional or local level of power, have consequences on global governance, on the understanding and the way to address limits and obstacles to economic and social development.

In addition to the two above mentioned characteristics, one of the most important challenges of the current world is fight against poverty. The present paper considers how regional and local authorities, can contribute to this fight against poverty, being given both the number of fields in which decentralised authorities have competency, due to decentralisation process, as well as the way they exert their competencies.

In that aim, it seems necessary to analyse the main issues associated to decentralised cooperation (3) before carrying out analysis of relations between decentralised cooperation and development policy (part 4). However, let's first consider factors explaining the increase in the decentralisation process (part 2) which in a large extent explains and promotes the development of decentralised cooperation.

2. Increasing decentralisation

All along the last twenty years, most of public decision actors, meaning international institutions, multilateral organisations, national government, regional and local authorities as well as civil society organisations are paying growing and substantial attention to decentralisation process. This later is indeed a clear and common trend in most of countries all around the world: towns, cities and other regional and local governments are being strengthened in a growing number of countries.

Empirically, various studies show that during the last decade both developing and developed countries exhibit if not absolutely similar, at least close trends. For example, considering a sample of 75 developing countries, Graham, Haggard and Willis[1] found that a large majority of them -84%- has been undergoing some decentralisation of authority. As regard to developed countries, Hooghe and Marks[2] identify that within the European Union, none of member states became more centralised since the beginning of the eighties, while many of them have decentralised authority to regional level of government.

The new forms of distribution of public authority have stimulated multiplication of new expressions. Among them are, for instance, polycentric governance, multi-perspectival governance and multi-level governance.

Obviously, any single factor can explain alone this above mentioned world-wide trend. Instead, many constituents enlighten this general movement towards a more important role of decentralised authorities.

2.1. Political explanations

Among them are notably political reasons. For example, in many countries, notably on Africa continent, the emergence of multi-party political system has created a movement in favour of a greater place for local voice in the decision

---

1 Graham C., Haggard S. and Willis E.J. (2001); Fiscal decentralization: A political Theory with American Cases; World Politics – volume 53, number 2.

2 Hooghes L & Marks G. (2001); Multi-Level Governance and European Integration, Lanham, MD: rowman and Littlefield. See also Hooghes L & Marks G. (2003); Contrasting Visions of Multi –level Governance; in Bache I. and Flinders M; eds; Multi Level Governance: Interdisciplinary Perspectives; Oxford University Press

making process. In that sense, decentralisation process appears as a consequence of important changes in electoral representative systems.

In others countries, in particular in former East European socialist states, decentralisation could mainly be explained by the fact that the previous centralised organisation was disintegrating. Within these countries, decentralisation appears in a large extent as the only meaningful and possible alternative to the decreasing role of central state.

In other supplementary cases, decentralisation, by granting more autonomy to all localities, occurs almost as an essential condition to maintain the country entity. Under these circumstances, sharing political power with regional and local authorities is the mean used to open participation to the government of the country to other groups and/or to political opposition.

Another important explanation to the growing decentralisation in many countries is associated to central government failure. Following this approach, decentralisation has happened as a consequence of the limits in capacities of central administrations. Many central governments have failed to provide required services not only to improve but even to maintain the quality of life of the majority of the population. Under these circumstances, extending decentralisation looks as the only meaningful alternative to provide many services to large part of populations[3].

In relation to the above point, one can note that central government failures undermine all the governance system in a country. They reduce the legitimacy of the whole state. In this way, decentralisation, generally associated with greater capacity to accurately provide services at regional and local level, can also be seen as a mean to increase legitimacy of the state as whole. In others words while on one side decentralisation diminished the central government power, on the other side it can also increase the governmental system legitimacy. In consequence, decentralisation process should not be seen as a local-versus-central phenomenon, but rather like a process in which both all authority levels and the population can take benefit.

2.2. Economic motivations

Among the major motives to decentralise, a growing share is based on the economic foundation of this process. While generally speaking, analyses investigate advantages as well as limits and difficulties associated with decentrelisation and mainly concentrate on the consequences of this process in terms of efficiency, macro-economic stabilisation and economic policy governance, activities carry out at regional and local levels usually appear to have specific and positive contribution to economic development. Furthermore, due partly to

---

3 See: http://www.ciesin.org/decentralisation/English/General/Rational/html

the relative failures of exclusively national development strategies and policies, regional and local actions also seem to be a potentially very well adapted tool for the fight against poverty.

One essential economic argument to support decentralisation is based on the idea that it can lead to a significant increase in efficiency. According the logic of this policy, central government is often too far away from most of needs and problems of citizens to provide good answers to all of them. The rationale is that public expenditures decided at level of government closer to local community have generally higher probability to accurately satisfy local demand than decision taken by a remote central authority. In other words, according this approach decentralisation is a good mean to improve global efficiency within the country as it allows a better allocation of factors and it provides for a better division of works among the different levels of government.

Fundamentally, regional and local government are considered to have greater potential to supply better services, and by the way to increase the global efficiency of all the administration. Among the justifications to this point are:

- Decentralisation contributes to reduce cost of actions as if "people feel that it is their money being spent, they are likely to keep tighter lid on expenditures and to use resources more efficiently"[4]. This reaction is easier and more straightforward to have with local government expenditures than with central authority activities.
- By comparison to central administration, policies decided and services provided by decentralised authorities can be more directly and more speedily adapted to special local conditions, to distinct regional needs. This greater capacity to adapt their activities is not only linked to the fact that decentralised authorities are more accessible, but is also associated with regional and local authorities' important knowledge about territorial situations. Finally, this capacity to customize their actions increases the chances of success of regional and local policies.
- Furthermore, development of decentralisation is potentially supporting greater transparency in public resources allocations as well as higher degree of accountability. Indeed, by bringing decision making nearer to people, decentralisation -at least- reduce possibilities for governments to misuse of power. This can lead to a better use of available funds and increase public administration efficiency because more responsibility is given to the level of government that represents most closely the beneficiaries of public expenditures.

A second important economic argument usually used in favour of decentralisation is based on the idea that citizens are keen to pay for services which are well matching up their priorities. In this case, decentralisation is viewed as a strategy to boost innovation as decentralised authorities try to adapt

---

4 UNDP (1993); Human Development Report.

their answers to specific regional and local conditions and search the most accurate solution in order to satisfy the wishes of citizens.

In relation with the previous one, a third well known rational for decentralisation is that it makes stronger regional and local authorities which can significantly help in improving local development projects. In some extent, there is here a kind of cumulative process connected to decentralisation. By improving capacities of decentralised entities, decentralisation makes it easier mobilisation and participation of regional and local resources to development strategy: it increases the ownership of the development strategy by decentralised actors. The same logic could also contribute to make more sustainable development policies including decentralised authorities within their design and implementation phases. Active participation to development strategy and actions facilitates regional and local authorities' long term attention and support.

2.3. Decentralisation: potential risks or limits

While it can be good response to many shortcomings of central governments and offers many more accurate answers to many problems, decentralisation is not the solution to solve all economic development problems. Whatever advantages it has, it cannot be regarded as the panacea for economic development. Basically, decentralisation can have various and opposite effects on social and economic conditions of one country.

Among the risks incurred with decentralisation is that, by contrast with central government, regional and local authorities are, almost by nature, less forced or pushed to consider the macro economic impact of their policies, while in the same time these policies can cause important and negative consequences on countries economic and social conditions. Are they intentional or not, decentralised authorities policies can affect country's macro economy performance and situation.

At macro-economic level, decentralisation can make harder both definition and implementation of sound political economy, notably stabilisation policy. One of the most underlined common dangers with decentralisation is indeed linked to the risk that it can result - in a rather easy or easier way- in significant increase in total public expenditures and debt. It is in particular the case when regional and local governments continuously increase their debt and when finally they cannot respect reimbursements, have to be refunded by central government. Argentina and in a certain extent Mexico have faced such described experiences.

Questions about equity are another major issue as regard to the potential impact of decentralisation. Essentially, difficulties can come from the existing imbalances in resources endowment between territories. Due to their geographical difference, size disparity, economic and physical location or historical factors, regional and local economies are generally not in equal situations. Some of them are in more disadvantaged conditions. Thus, it is often necessary, even only for economic reasons or for efficiency purposes, to decide a policy aiming at – at least - reducing inequalities. It is clear that such a policy cannot be elaborated exclusively at regional and local levels. Central state authority has also to intervene to reduce disparities between lagging and advanced territories.

Always on economic ground, decentralisation can also negatively impact public authorities' conditions in providing services. Specifically, decentralisation, can lower if not eliminate opportunities for economies of scale. To put it in other words, development of decentralisation or expansion of decentralised authorities' power also mean increase in number of service providers, and -ceteris paribus- in consequence increase in the average cost of providing services. Similarly, multiplication of production sites can imply, in case of lack of coordination among decentralised authorities that many of them try to (re)invent the same wheel.

Fundamentally, the above mentioned risks and limits underline how important are the decentralisation conditions. Decentralisation considered as a political project aiming at increasing regional and local levels participation can correspond with the economic objectives of better decisions about the use of public funds. To successfully fulfil its objectives, decentralisation process required in fact some essential conditions[5]. Among them are (i) the central state commitment to decentralise and share power with regional and local governments; (ii) Capacity and willingness of policy makers to ensure an actual decentralisation process; (iii) the availability of sufficient resources and the possibility for decentralised authorities of using these resources autonomously; and (iv) actual principle of accountability, meaning that clear responsibility and rules of conduct as well as high transparency are required in the distribution of competencies between the various government levels.

3. Enlargement of Decentralised cooperation

In relation with the increasing decentralisation, meaning the growing power of local and regional authorities, the later have also developed during the last decades their international relations.

Essentially, the international relations and actions of decentralised authorities, nowadays, actually embrace many aspects. Firstly, let's consider that in addition to actions for better social and economic environment, i.e. in some extent actions aiming at improving the attraction of the territory, including vis-à-vis international partners, international actions of regional and local authorities incorporate promotion of their territory on international scenes, contain a kind of

---

5 See: http://www.ciesin.org/decentralisation/English/General/Rational/html

international marketing of the territory. This promotion has been for a long time done for tourism purposes; advertising regional and local tourist advantages. However, it cannot be restrained to this sector or to this dimension, in the extent that today territorial promotion also includes promotion of the economic, social, environmental strengths and advantages of the territory. As Regard to the economic aspects, it aims in particular to attract investors, including international investors, i.e. supplier of foreign direct investments.

A second increasing aspect of the internationalisation of local and regional authorities' actions is given by the growing number of foreign offices opened by decentralised authorities'. While few of them are simply acting as representative offices and propose few basic services, others are more committed to territorial interests protection, territorial promotion or/and development of international trade with their territory, notably via administrative and technical supports proposed to businessman.

Thirdly, one of the most important development as regard to the internationalisation of local and regional authorities activities during the last decades is probably exceptional increase in decentralised cooperation operations. In order to better analyse this point (3.2) it seem first necessary to give more precise definition of this phenomenon (3.1).

3.1. Definitions of decentralised cooperation.

Initiated around the end of the seventies and the first years of the eighties, the concept or term of 'Decentralized Cooperation' is relatively young, and try to describe a recent but growing phenomenon. Basically, decentralized cooperation can be considered as an evolving concept based on two pillars: development cooperation and international relations carry out by and/or with decentralised entities.

Indeed, despite or because its relatively recent emergence, the concept of decentralised cooperation can covers very different meanings according the various actors involved in this kind of operations. One of the major differences is precisely associated to the variety of entities which should be considered among the actors of the decentralised cooperation.

According to a first approach supported by some European Union member states, as France, decentralised cooperation refers specifically to cooperation for development carried out singularly or in consortium, by regional and local institutions from one country in favour of regional and local institutions that needs support, in another and third country. In a large extent, this view of decentralised cooperation expresses north-south solidarity and exchange objectives at territorial authorities' level.

Following another conception, supported for example by Italy as well as by the European commission, decentralised cooperation involves much more extensive number of participants and activities. Precisely, it is now considered as including not only all actions perform between regional and local authorities but also covers cooperation activities achieve by non state actors. Among the entities generally considered as non state actors are for instance; non governmental organisations (NGOs); cooperatives; unions; churches and religious associations; professional associations; cooperatives; consumers associations; universities; cultural, scientific, research organisations; local associations (see: Box 1).

However, even if for policy and political purposes the two groups – local and regional authorities and non states actors- should not be mixed, in practise the two above mentioned approaches of decentralised cooperation are nowadays actually closer and closer. Indeed, decentralised cooperation is increasingly becoming a territory to territory cooperation. In consequence, regional and local authorities are developing their activities more and more in association or in partnership with numerous regional and local civil society organisations. The two categories of actors are more complementary than any other things in cooperation for territorial economic and social development.

Thus, decentralized cooperation embodies a broad range of local entities from civil society in both donor and beneficiary countries. It means involving local authorities, various bodies representing civil society, cooperatives, NGOs, the grey economy and private sector firms. It aims to meet the challenges of development and cooperation policies more effectively (e.g. alleviation of poverty, strengthening civil society, local development) and increase the impact of aid and cooperation activities. The present paper adopts the last definition of decentralisation cooperation, even if the analysis is mainly focusing on the role of regional and local authorities.

3.2. Origin of decentralised cooperation.

Decentralised cooperation can be seen as the successor, or the logical step following twinning agreements between cities.

In 1950, Montbélliard and Ludwigsburg conclude the first twinning agreement among cities, respectively, from France and from Germany. By the way, years before the signature of the Rome treaty, they paved the way for new intra European relations. In some extend, with cities twining, local authorities initiate European reconciliation built on involvement and commitment of decentralised authorities

Box 1: Civil society organisations, Non-governmental Organisations and Non State Actors.

Civil society organisations regroup very different associations organised to express the point of view, act on behalf of and represent various categories of persons or sectors. The World Bank uses this term of civil society to identify a wide array of non-governmental and not-for-profit organisations that have a presence in public life, expressing the interests and values of their members or others, based on ethical, cultural, political, scientific, religious or philanthropic considerations.

Non-governmental organisations (NGO) are part - sub-group - of civil society organisations. They are any non-profit, voluntary citizen's groups which are organised on a local, national or international level. They include groups that have primarily humanitarian or cooperative rather commercial objectives.

Non state actors indicate organisations which put together civil society organisations - apart from governmental and public administration. They usually include NGO, social partners, schools, universities, social partners, private sector association but also profit organisation.

During the seventies, decentralised authorities initiated another kind of international relations; specifically they concluded new categories of twinning. The latter were mainly concluded between European and African cities and demonstrate new kind of relations between these cities consecutive to access to the independence of numerous African countries. This geographical change in twinning has instigated fundamental modifications in the nature of the relations between cities. During the last decades, decentralised cooperation has changes both in quantitative and qualitative terms. On one side, there was a clear increase in the number of actors and actions. On the other side, one can also note that while previously, international decentralised relations were mainly based on exchange in cultural and sports activities they became more and more associated to cooperation for development.

Since this initial step, donors, beneficiaries, and most of the other actors in cooperation for development are paying greater and greater attention to decentralised cooperation.

Basically, two major -linked- factors explain this trend all along the last decades. Firstly, with expansion of the decentralisation process, regional and local authorities are becoming more autonomous and are developing their specific advantages. In relation with these trends, decentralised public authorities are also increasing their international relations, including notably their development cooperation activities. These new cooperation for development fields opened to regional and local authorities generally appear as the international extension of their growing national competencies.

Secondly, the relative lacks or deficiencies in international cooperation with central governments give support to new approaches in cooperation for development and international relations. Traditional cooperation for development, mainly organised on a country to country logic has not fully succeeded in reducing poverty which is the actual objective of European Union and others donors' development policies. Thus, and in relation with the previous point, it appears appropriate and pertinent to consider specific opportunities, advantages and value added brought by decentralised cooperation policies and operations.

The increasing attention and consideration paid to decentralised cooperation in many fora found one of the first, if not the first explicit and official international recognition in 1992. Indeed, the specific character of – international- actions carried out by regional and local authorities' was underlined at the United Nations Conference on Environment and Development, better known as the Earth Summit. Held in Rio de Janiero, this unprecedented Summit was mainly dedicated to environment and sustainable development issues. It resulted in particular in the adoption by the world leaders of the United Nations framework Convention on Climate Change[6] and of the so called Agenda 21. The latter is a comprehensive programme for actions to achieve sustainable development worldwide. The Chapter 28 of this Agenda 21 asked every local authority in the world to contribute and support this Agenda 21: It is the Local Agenda 21[7]. More recently, in 2004, the United Nations Development Programme (UNDP) has launch a new programme, named ART-GOLD – for "support to territorial and thematic networks of human development cooperation". It intends to help regional and local authorities to conclude agreements and partnerships in support of local development and governance processes.

At the European Union (EU) level, the primary and formal reference to the contribution of regional and local authorities to international relations was

6 It led to the Kyoto protocol open for signature on 11 December 1997.

7 Often shortened to LA21

associated to cooperation for development which is one of the main objectives of the decentralised cooperation[8].

Specifically, the first reference to the principle of "decentralised cooperation" at the EU level was established within the Lomé IV Convention, in 1989. That convention, concluded between the African, Caribbean and Pacific (ACP) Group of States and the EU sets up in its article 20 that "in order to encourage all parties from the ACP States and the Community which are in a position to contribute to the autonomous development of the ACP States to put forward and implement initiatives, cooperation shall also support, within limits laid down by the ACP States concerned, development operations put forward by economic, social and cultural organizations in the framework of decentralized cooperation, in particular where they combine the efforts and resources of organizations from the ACP States and their counterparts from the Community. This form of cooperation shall be aimed in particular at making the capabilities, original operating methods and resources of such parties available to the development of the ACP States."

Since this major step, many other texts mention co-operation activities performed by regional and local authorities and include special provision as regard to these activities. For instance, the first European Union regulation on decentralised cooperation, in July 1998, stated that "decentralised cooperation is a new approach to development cooperation which places the agents at the focal point of implementation and hence pursues the dual aims of gearing operations to needs and making them viable."[9]

At cooperation programme level, various initiatives also took place during the nineties. For example, URB-AL and Asia-URBS programmes intend to support decentralised cooperation with two different partner zones. Precisely, they aim at developing decentralised cooperation between regional and local authorities from European Union and –respectively- Latin America as well as Asia countries.

---

8 However, it should be noted that during the first part of the eighties, the Council of Europe initiates two texts establishing the right for regional and local authorities to develop co-operation with the homologous authorities in other countries. Firstly, in 1980, the European outline convention on trans-frontier co-operation between territorial communities or authorities, as well as two Additional Protocols recognising the right for local and regional authorities to co-operate across frontiers in providing public services and environmental protection. Secondly, on 15 October 1985, The European Charter of Local self Government setting out the principle that effective local self-government is essential to democracy. These two initiates have more than probably influenced changes introduced in others forum, including at the EU level and in its Member States.

See: http://www.coe.int/t/congress/4-Texts/conventions_en.asp.

9 Council regulation N°1659/98; OJEC L213/6; 30th July.

More recently, among the main amendments introduced in 2005 within the Cotonou agreement[10] concludes between the EU and the ACP states are those related to local authorities. The new Article 4 of this agreement asserts that "the parties recognise the complementary role of and potential for contributions by non state actors and local decentralised authorities to the development process". While the previous version of this article did not explicitly mentioned local decentralised authorities.

In the same vein, the 2005 revision of Cotonou agreement also introduces eligibility for financial support to the benefit of local decentralised authorities from ACP states and from the Community. Essentially, this 2005 revised version of the Cotonou agreement incorporates the explicit recognition of decentralised authorities as full partners in the EU-ACP countries' relations. Decentralised authorities are not merely possible beneficiaries of programmes; instead they are now actors of the partnership.

Proposed in 2005 and adopted in 2006, the "European Consensus" [11] for development confirms and in some extent generalises the trend asserted by the 2005 revision of the Cotonou agreement. Indeed, the European Consensus establishes that ownership and partnership of development cooperation strategies and programmes by partner countries are key principles of the EU policies vis-à-vis developing countries. In order to promote these principles, the European consensus notifies that "the EU encourages increased involvement of official institutions that represent society, in particular [...] local authorities."[12]

The recently created EU instrument for development cooperation[13] (DCI), valuable at least for the 2007-2013 period, shows another important step in the same direction. It initiates the thematic programme "non state actors and local authorities in development"[14] which aims at (a) facilitating their participation in poverty reduction and sustainable development strategies; (b) strengthening their capacity, (c) supporting coordination and communication activities of non state actors and local authorities. In that purpose, up to 15% of the amount reserved for this thematic programme will be allocated to decentralised authorities. In other words, during the 2007-2013 period, the annual budget potentially

---

10 Formally or officially, it is the "Partnership Agreement concluded between the members of the African, Caribbean and pacific Group of states of the part one and the European Community and its Member States of the other part". It was signed in Cotonou on 21 June 2000.

11 EU Official Journal (2006); Joint declaration by the Council, the European Parliament and the Commission on the European Union Development Policy; C 46.

12 Idem

13 European Parliament and Council (2006); Regulation N° 1905/2006 establishing a financing instrument for development cooperation.

14 COM(2006) 19

available for activities of local authorities linked to decentralised cooperation policy and/or projects is around 32 millions euros.

In accordance with international and EU changes about decentralised cooperation, most of the EU Member states have also acted in order to support international cooperation carried out by regional and local authorities. In that aim they decided, during the last decades, to maintain, reinforce or elaborate new institutional and legal frameworks in order to take into account or allow the increase in decentralised cooperation operations.

Formally, the right to carry out an active role during both planning and implementation phases of cooperation activities for development is recognised to Italian territorial authorities since 1987. Similarly, in 1992 and 2005, the French government has laid down a new framework for the action of French local authorities. In particular these French laws recognised the right for the country's territorial authorities to conclude conventions with foreign territorial entities. Local authorities have autonomy in decentralised development cooperation with their counterparts in other countries. These laws appear as the ultimate phases of a process started ten years before with an important set of decentralisation laws. Other examples of innovative and recent laws on decentralised cooperation in EU member states are given by Austria and Spain. They have both adopted new judicial frameworks in 1998[15].

Finally, at least within the European Union and whatever the background and justification associated with the definition and concept retained for its identification, decentralised cooperation seems to present for all actors number of points of convergence. This suggests common and shared characteristics involving (a) presence and preponderance of local actors (including obviously regional and local authorities), (b) a fundamental objective (sustainable –local-economic and social development) and (c) to carry out activities based on cooperation and support for which exchanges of experiences, resources and ideas are in many cases taking place.

3.3. Decentralised cooperation in practice

Despite the increasing contribution of decentralised authorities to international cooperation for development, statistical information about their actual achievements remains erratic. National practices and methods of declaration are

---

15 For compilation about EU Member States' legal framework on decentralised cooperation; see :

- Burger P. (2006); Coopération décentralisée et lutte contre la désertification, CARI.

- OCDE (2005): Aide allouée par les collectivités territoriales; Tiré-à-part des Dossiers du CAD, volume 6, N°4.

relatively different from one country to another and in consequence, compilation and international comparisons are essentially difficult.

In term of quantity, measured by the amount spend by decentralised authorities for cooperation activities carried out by regional and local entities are very different among the member states. The amount spent by European Union decentralised entities are highly variables. In absolute terms, it can fluctuate within a ratio from 1 to more than 1000, according member state.

Furthermore, while it can be considered as almost negligible or very weak in some member states, decentralised cooperation account for a very significant part of the country total public aid in other member states. For example, in 2002-2003, while decentralised cooperation fund explain less than 0.1 percent in Greece bilateral public development aid, the equivalent figure in Spain is 18 percent[16].

According the data available, decentralised cooperation funds appear to be actually significant in three EU countries. They are, in increasing order: Belgium (5%), Germany (11%) and Spain (18%). Shares of local and regional authorities relatively to total public aid in Italy and Austria are also to be considered: they respectively equal around 2% and 1% of the country total public aid for development.

While the above results broadly show a relatively limited participation of local and regional authorities in public aid for development, one should not conclude that decentralised cooperation activities are unimportant in most countries. Indeed, various factors allow another understanding, among them are:

Firstly, as seen previously the actual and active development of decentralised cooperation is a relatively young process. In consequence it is probably not yet fully implemented and developed.

Secondly, while local and regional authorities generally account for a relatively modest part of the public aid for development, it has to be noted that their contribution is almost everywhere growing in absolute and relative terms. For instance, in Spain, during the last fifteen years decentralised cooperation increased from 2.1 % to around 18% of the total public aid for development, without reduction of the later.

Thirdly, it should be noted that the above results describe decentralised cooperation exclusively as regard to one single indicator: the amount spend by local and regional authorities. This creates shortcomings as many projects can be carried out with a limited amount of direct fund. In particular, most activities aiming at capacity building are not taken into account as they are frequently implemented with in kind transfer. Following the same logic, cooperation based on partnership and exchange of experiences are not accurately covered with the public aid indicator.

---

16 Data are from OECD (2005), op.cit.

In sectoral terms, local and regional authorities appear to concentrate their actions mainly in social sectors. Approximately 70% of the amount spent in decentralised cooperation activities are in these sectors.

Specifically, education services -in particular secondary school and professional training- is the first sector for public aid from Austrian, Belgian and German local and regional authorities. While decentralised cooperation from Italy and Spain are for the most important part developed, respectively, in health services and in "infrastructure and other social services".

In a large extend this kind of specialisation in social sector services is not surprising. In fact, it appears as a logical consequence of the institutional and judicial framework of decentralised cooperation. Indeed, even if decentralised authorities can perform very different international actions according countries, they usually have a clear competency in social sector services in most countries.

As regard to the spatial distribution of decentralised cooperation activities, two factors appear to be very influential. One is the direction of public aid for development at national or central state level. The other is, in relation with the first one, the historical and cultural links existing among countries and their decentralised entities. For instance Belgium decentralised authorities develop their operations manly in favour of African partners. While supports offer by Spanish territorial authorities primarily go to Latin America. Similarly, Decentralised development cooperation in Africa accounts for 53% of French local authority cooperation projects.

4. Decentralised cooperation and development policy

4.1. Governance and development

Development policy aim, including obviously at the EU level, is to reduce and ultimately to eliminate poverty. However, until now, despite undeniable achievements, the global result in the fight against poverty remains unsatisfactory. It the reason why, one of the eight objectives of the Millennium Development Goals endorsed by United Nations Members States is to eradicate extreme poverty and hunger[17].

The Millennium Development Goals also underlines the important issue related to governance. Countries must set their strategy to ensure that people benefit from development. In other words, meeting the ambitious goals include within the Millennium declaration requires good governance. In full coherence with the Unites Nations approach, the European development policy also gives

17 Specifically, considering the target date of 2015, the proportion of people living on less than a dollar a day and the proportion of people who suffer from hunger, should be reduced by half.

great importance to governance issue. Precisely, institutional capacities building, particularly in the area of good governance and rule of law is one of the six priority fields of the European Community development policy.

The term of "governance" is used in several social sciences and has various meanings. Until now there is no international agreed and shared special definition of this word and -a fortiori- there are different approaches to identify good governance (Box 2). At the European Union level, the concept of governance was initially established within the European Commission white paper on European governance published in July 2001. According the document, the concept of governance "refers to the rules, processes and behaviour that affect the way in which powers are exercised at European level, particularly as regards openness, participation, accountability, effectiveness and coherence. These five "principles of good governance" reinforce those of subsidiarity and proportionality".[18]

Box 2: Assessing governance: many approaches[19]

Good governance is a challenge to quantify and measure. The attempts vary dramatically in what is measured. Some of these attempts and their definitions of good governance include:

- *Country policy and institutional assessments*. The World Bank Country policy and institutional assessments cover policy choices and institutional structures. They evaluate economic management (debt, macroeconomic and fiscal policies), structural policies (trade, financial, private sector strategy), policies for social inclusion and equity and public sector management and institutions (rules of law, financial management, efficiency of public administration, transparency, accountability, corruption).

- *Freedom House*. The Freedom in the world rankings use surveys to measure political freedom and civil liberties. Political freedom are measured by the right to vote, compete for public office, and elect representatives who have a decisive vote on public policies. Civil liberties include the freedom to develop opinions, institutions, and personal autonomy without interference from the state.

- *International Country Risk Guide*. It ranks countries based on political, economic and financial risks. Political risk includes government stability, socioeconomic conditions, investment profile, corruption, conflict,

18 European Commission (2001), European Governance a White Paper; COM(2001) 428 final.

19 From: UN Report Millennium Project (2005) ; Chapter 7: Governance to achieve the Millennium Development Goals; In: Investing in Development: a Practical Plan to Achieve the Millennium Development Goals.

quality of bureaucracy, democratic accountability, law and order, and the presence of religion and the military in government. Economic risk measurements include per capita GDP, GDP growth, inflation, official reserves and exchange rate stability.

- *Kaufmann, Kraay and Zoido-lobaton & Kaufmann, Kraay and Mastruzzi.* These data sets, produced by the global governance group at the World Bank institute, rank countries based on six aspects of governance: voice and accountability, political stability, absence of violence, government effectiveness, regulatory quality, rule of law and control of corruption.

- *Millennium challenge account.* It was announced by the U.S. government in 2002 as a new foreign aid programme to assist countries that are relatively well governed. Governance is measured based on three broad categories: ruling justly, investing in people and encouraging economic freedoms. Ruling justly is measured by score on civil liberties, political freedoms, voice and accountability, government effectiveness, rule of law, and control of corruption. Investing in people is measured by public spending devoted to health and education, primary completion rates, and immunization rates. Encouraging economic freedoms is measured by fiscal and trade balances and the investor climate.

- *Transparency international.* It ranks countries on the basis of a corruption perception index, a composite index that measures the degree to which corruption is perceived to exist among public officials and politicians.

4.2. Towards multi-levels governance

As already mentioned, major characteristics of the current world include both globalisation and decentralisation. In such a world, public policies are essential in order to provide answer to the major challenge of poverty eradication. In that sense, to be able to deal both with the world problems and grassroots one, contributions from all levels of power are necessary. While poverty reduction strategies are supported by economic growth and greater integration of developing countries within the world economy, they cannot be reached only as result of these policies.

In other words, in our contemporary world it is essential to develop complementary in policies and actions of all authorities are they at international, EU, national, regional, local or civil society level. It's the reason the governance issue is also a multi-levels governance issue: important improvements in global governance imply both greater participation of local and regional entities within the process and better coordination between all decision levels.

The need for interactive and well organised relations among all levels of authorities is important not only for countries' internal policies, but also for their international affairs. In a large extent, the international dimensions of activities developed by regional and local authorities complete and extend their internal roles.

Many arguments support the need to extend and deepen multi-levels governance. Firstly, it should be noted fact that one essential aspect of multi-levels governance is linked to the degree of local and regional authorities' involvement in policy decision process. Specifically, concrete and important participation of decentralised entities from policy and strategy definitions to implementation and evaluation phases appears as essential in order to increase policy appropriation. Indeed, in the extent that decentralised authorities are close to population they greater integration to decision process is a way to increase opportunity for voices and concerns of the poor are better represented and taken into account within policies. This contributes to ease implementation of policies and improves their global efficiency. In consequence, supporting appropriation of the development policy, i.e. supporting capacity of developing countries to be decision makers and ultimately responsible for their development supposes capacity building for each level of authority.

Secondly, development of multi-levels governance is also to be encouraged, because it allows a greater flexibility in project planning and implementation. Even when national development policy is well shaped, it could be necessary to adapt implementation, at local and/or regional level(s), according existing specific conditions. In that sense, a major advantage brought by multi-level governance is to avoid the so called "one size fits all" policies. By the way it also broadens the number of actors that are involved in development process and in consequence is reducing the central government monopoly. This -partial- transfer of responsibility participates to a broader movement in favour of democracy and fight against corruption[20].

Thirdly, enhanced multi-levels governance is required as appropriate answer to the increase in decentralisation and in decentralised cooperation operations. This change almost necessarily results in a multiplication of actors involved in development process and promoting initiatives, proposals and projects which have to be integrated in a general or national development policy. In consequence, it becomes crucial to create adapted means and instruments in order to guarantee global coherence among parties and actions. Thus, coherent institutional framework and good coordination practices between partners are key factors.

---

20 Vashee B. (1997); Revitalising EU-ACP Cooperation : How Decentralised Cooperation can Contribute to Poverty Eradication in Africa; Issues paper prepared for the Summit of ACP Heads of State and Government.

4.3. Improving cooperation and development policies

As previously noted, specific advantages and inputs introduced by local and regional authorities in development and cooperation policies is nowadays legitimated in almost all fora, are they multilateral, pluri-lateral, international, national or sub national.

For example one of the innovations of the last revision of Cotonou agreement is to allow participation of decentralised authorities -as well as non state actors- in cooperation programmes definition. This approach is the going in the right direction. It enlarges the social base needed to successfully achieved reforms as acceptance by the population is in many case a crucial factor.

In fact, during the last ten years the European community has undertaken efforts to elaborate a development policy including or based on participative approach. The 2002 European commission communication on "participation of non states actors in the EC development policy"[21] demonstrates the will and means to involve non-states actors and -in a lesser extent- decentralised authorities in the European development policy.

The European consensus, published in 2005, confirms the growing legitimacy of regional and local authorities in European development policy and the specific added value of decentralised cooperation. However, despite improvements expressed on theoretical side, the empirical or practical side remains difficult. Participation and contribution of local and regional authorities within the development policy definition remain reduced both in developing countries and in developed countries

In order to correct this trend and to introduce, on practical ground, means to fully implement the above approach it seems necessary to consider at least the establishment of two innovations.

Firstly, special attention should be given to a double dimension as regard to the local and regional authorities' participation in development policy. One dimension is the absolute need to include in each development strategy, policies and actions decided and to be implemented at the levels and/or with decentralised authorities. The other dimension should incorporate policies, operations and assistances that should be better developed via decentralised cooperation. Obviously, according the beneficiary country and decentralised authorities competencies cooperation priorities will differs, but this approach will allows to take advantage from the fact that it is clear nowadays that some policies are better designed and implemented at regional or local levels that at central authority level. Specifically within the European community, such an approach could be done by incorporating decentralised development policy and

21 European Comission (2002) ; COM(2002) 598

decentralised cooperation in each country strategic paper and national indicative programme.

Secondly, the appropriation objective by developing countries implies a greater involvement of decentralised entities in policies definition. This implies in many cases an increasing demand for capacity building, a growth in assistance and a proliferation of projects which could be linked to the rise in decentralised cooperation activities. As a consequence, it becomes more and more important to coordinate actions undertaken by various donors: this could be called coordination of the supply side. The same logic is also relevant on the demand or beneficiary side as the later are confront to -and have to manage- a growing number of actions, putting their management capacities under difficulties. Establishing a coordination system aiming better coherence among donors acting in favour the same partner will ease the appropriation of the development policy by the beneficiaries of aid.

Literature

Bossuyt J. and Gould J. (2000): Decentralisation and Poverty Reduction: Elaborating the Linkages; Policy Management Brief, N°12, ECDPM, Maastricht, the Netherlands

Burger P. (2006); Coopération décentralisée et lutte contre la désertification, CARI.

European Commission (2000): communication on the European Community Development Policy; COM(2000) 212 final.

European Commission (2001), European Governance a White Paper; COM(2001) 428 final.

European Commission (2002): Participation of non-state actors in EC development policy; COM(2002) 598 final.

European Commission (2005): European Development Policy "The European Consensus" COM(2005) 311 final.

Gilly J.P.; Wallet F. (2001): Forms of proximity, local governance and the dynamics of local economic spaces: the case of industrial conversion process; International and Regional Research, September.

Galasso E and Ravallion M. (2004): Decentralized Targeting of an Anti-Poverty Program; Journal of Public Economics N° 89 (4).

Graham C., Haggard S. and Willis E.J. (2001); Fiscal decentralization: A political Theory with American Cases; World Politics – volume 53, number 2.

Hooghes L & Marks G. (2001); Multi-Level Governance and European Integration, Lanham, MD: rowman and Littlefield. See also Hooghes L & Marks G. (2003); Contrasting Visions of Multi –level Governance; in Bache I. and Flinders M; eds; Multi Level Governance: Interdisciplinary Perspectives; Oxford University Press

Kaiser K. (2006): Decentralization Reforms; in Coudouel A. and Paternostro S. (Editors): Analysing the Distributional Impact of Reforms; Poverty & Social Impact Analysis; vol. 2.

Kälin W. (2000): Decentralization: Why and How?; University of Berne; Berne; Switzerland.

Fukusaku K. and De Mello L.R. (1999): Fiscal Decentralisation in Emerging Economies; OECD Development Centre Seminars, Paris.

Marie A. (2005): La coopération décentralisée et ses paradoxes. Dérives bureaucratiques et notabiliaires du développement local en Afrique ; Paris, Karthala.

OECD (2005): Aide allouée par les collectivités territoriales; Tiré-à-part des Dossiers du CAD, volume 6, N°4.

OECD (2004)-(a): Ownership and Partnership: What Role for Civil Society in Poverty Reduction Strategies?; Paris.

Jütting J., Kauffmannn C., Mc Donnell I. and Alii (2004): Decentralisation and poverty in developing countries: exploring the impact; OECD Development Centre, Working Paper N° 236, August, Paris.

Ter-Minassian T. (1997): Decentralizing Government; Finances & Development, September.

UNDP (2004); Decentralised Governance for Development: A combined Practice note on Decentralisation, Local governance and Urban/rural Development.

UN Report Millennium Project (2005) ; Investing in Development: a Practical Plan to Achieve the Millennium Development Goals.

Andreas Weida

Concepts of a local business tax - an overview of criteria and arguments

1. Introduction

A local business tax (LBT) is a tax falling on private enterprises, including partnerships, the revenue of which goes to the relevant local authorities (i.e. municipalities, counties or similar "lower" tiers of government).

There are different suggestions which tax base seems most appropriate at the local level, be that the current revenue of the enterprise, the cash flow, the total capitalised assets, the property, the wage bill or the profit. The tax itself can either be established as being deductible from the income tax in a combined system or be fully separate in a "classical" system.

In a situation where rivalry on business location and firm registration continues within and between countries, the pressure to lower business taxes has led to a discussion on different models in order to avoid a total erosion of revenues for the authorities involved and the necessity to cut down consequently their public services for the population.[1] This problem is aggravated by the well-known fact that central municipalities normally have to provide services, mostly infrastructure services that are also used by enterprises and citizens of adjacent municipalities which do not automatically pay for these services via their tax bill.

For most EU Member States local taxes on companies form a standard part of the tax receipts. However, as the problems of inequalities and tax competition have risen, there were a number of reform measures taken or at least discussed.[2] Among those have figured the deletion of existing taxes on equity or on total aggregate capital, maintaining for example only the tax on profits, the harmonisation of the tax (that is tax rate and/or tax base) on profit and/or cash-flow at a higher (national) level as well as the substitution of the standard local business tax with a right for local authorities to raise a surcharge on a centrally administered corporate income tax. However, given that the basic problem of erosion does not differ from the discussion on the corporate income tax, a solution with a formula apportionment of the tax base maintaining the right to set different tax rates would in principle also be possible.

---

1 Cf. Eggert, W.; Haufler, A. (2006); p. 10. on the studies dealing with the effect of a shift to a stronger taxation of immobile factors as a (negative) consequence.

2 See the overview in Sterdyniak, H. (2005): Taxation in Europe, towards more competition or more co-ordination, OFCE Working Paper, No.2005-19, p.21-22.

The model of a surcharge on the corporate income tax (or in the case of partnerships personal income tax of the firm owner) has to be strictly separated from the notion of regionalizing other central taxes, notably the income tax on every person (including house owners, workers and people receiving interest incomes/capital gains).However, insights from the discussions of the income tax can have repercussions on the debate on an appropriate LBT.

Furthermore it is not the purpose here to discuss to what extent tax receipts could be replaced by user fees (especially for infrastructure, education, libraries) as both ways of financing have always existed side-by-side and as a total replacement seems unrealistic. It is still worthwhile to concentrate on requirements for an efficient method to raise taxes alone.

2. Criteria for tax comparison

The standard literature normally discusses at least two principles, the benefit principle (Äquivalenzprinzip in German) and the ability to pay-principle (Leistungsfähigkeitsprinzip in German) as a focus for tax comparisons. Apart from those, other criteria can also be helpful for assessing different concepts of a LBT. As a standard procedure, this can be done in a neoclassical framework using general equilibrium theory. There is no need to distinguish further at this stage between standard neoclassical or Keynesian approaches because all neoclassical frameworks can respect in principle the right of the state to collect taxes as such, can accept a tax "wedge" as at least an unavoidable distortion when compared to results under totally free competition and thus they can acknowledge the right of the state to correct market failure (through more or less interventionist measures) and to help market development.

As classical concepts that do not operate with general equilibrium theory - for example those of radical liberal or of Marxist origin - and other economic concepts (e.g. evolutionary theory) are rarely used for tax comparisons, we do not take them into consideration here either. However, one has to bear in mind that every evaluation of the relevance of certain criteria could in principle be challenged on the grounds that the underlying economic model is not undisputed.

2.1. Benefit principle

The benefit principle stipulates that those who pay the taxes and those who benefit from the public goods should be more or less the same group. By doing so, the solution of the allocative problem by tax financing would be the closest to a solution by fees, thus to a market-like solution. This way of tax collection and attribution of benefits would consequently be as efficient as possible, accepting of course a certain redistributive element of a tax as such.

Proponents of this principle acknowledge that a state intervention may be necessary for public goods, which in a technical sense cannot be provided by enterprises,[3] but that on the financing side the state should nevertheless approach a market solution as closely as possible, because the market and price system is deemed to be the most efficient.

However, given that the redistribution of income is not a side-effect of taxation but the core of any tax system in market economies, it seems doubtful from the outset that the benefit principle to give the benefit principle a central place as a criterion. This is even more valid for a LBT that derives its sense from the fact that some of the extra burden that companies impose for a local community (e.g. infrastructure requirements, waste management) should be paid for. Taxes exist in order to redistribute, otherwise one should rather advocate fees.[4]

The notion of equivalency is however helpful, when mainly interpreted not in the personal, but in the spatial sense, that means that the benefits of a tax collected from the local community A should not go the inhabitants of community B. But even in this regard the benefit principle should gain only secondary importance as a criterion compared with the "ability to pay"-principle. Actually, there are a number of policies, including focused tax reductions or direct cohesion instruments (for example the EU structural funds) that also redistribute between territories and are not necessarily targeting the absolutely poorest population in the poorer region. So, if one accepts cohesion policy and

3 In a political context it is sufficient to note that a certain good possesses some of the criteria of a public good and that it would be technically more difficult to provide it via the market. It is not necessary to show that it is absolutely "technically" impossible to provide it via private market participants. In this sense, all modern public goods are to some extent "chosen" public goods. The population has voted in favour of a non-market supply after having acknowledged the pros and cons of each solution along the lines of public goods theory.

4 The benefits principle is advocated from (radical) neoclassical schools arguing that the ability-to-pay principle could not be respected as it would not be known who would ultimately bear higher prices (ultimate tax incidence) etc.. The idea that taxes do fall on people and not on business is however unconvincing (see in this regard Oakland, W.; Testa, (1998): Can the benefits principle be applied to state-local taxation of business ? Working Paper Series 16-98; Federal Reserve Bank of Chicago); when the same school of thought argues on the other hand in favour of consumption taxes, because consumption should be taxed and not the possibility to consume (income). In the end also consumption taxes would fall on groups of people, not on consumption. Furthermore real tax incidence is always difficult to determine. If a capital tax diminishes the income of shareholders at the first stage, it is practically what was intended and expected, whether this leads to higher prices, lower employment etc. is dependant on a large number of conditions. But that is also true of any other policy measure (e.g. R&D subsidies, tax cuts or an import ban on ivory) and no reason to abandon the ability-to-pay principle in favour of the benefit principle.

its dominant twofold objectives, that is encouraging growth potentials and levelling out chances throughout a greater territorial community, there is not so much room for a benefit principle as a decisive criterion for a LBT within the comparison of tax concepts.

2.2. Ability to pay-principle

The "ability to pay"- principle derives from the fact that one common result of the market mechanism is an uneven income distribution, sometimes with extreme differences. In order to make the market system acceptable to the "worse-off" classes and individuals, any redistributive policy should work in a way that public goods are financed through taxes predominantly collected from the better-off citizens, that is those that have gained through their activity within a predominantly market system.

It has to be stressed that the "choice for a market system" accompanied by a compensation to those who would have voted for a different system can only be incorporated into a general equilibrium framework and surely not into classical liberal concepts. The classical liberal cannot understand the notion of "choice" of a system plus a compensation for those who have voted (or would have voted) against, because the installation of a market system is in this theory given "for free" and advocated as a principle. In classical concepts, market-like relationships are regarded as reflecting fundamental "individual" formal liberty and do not need a societal justification. However, once the idea is accepted that a market system is not "for free" but implies costs and benefits like any other economic decision, the ability-to-pay principle receives an additional theoretical backing.[5] The ability to pay principle furthermore runs diametrically against the "incentive to work" principle currently discussed for redirecting the scope and concept income transfers, where the capability of adaptation to market principles is receiving a premium.

The ability-to-pay principle has certain clear advantages that normally make it figure amongst the most central criteria:

---

5 It has to be pointed out that neoclassical theory derives the relative superiority of a market system from the starting condition of individual utility maximisation. For a person who would individually be better off in a different system, there would then still be the problem that he is totally rational when voting against the socially optimal system (because he is within this theory not a social optimizer). For that reason moderate neoclassicals can accept that the possibility to compensate out of the efficiency gains is sufficient to justify the "choice" of a market system. This compensation to certain individuals ("losers" in a market system) is then carried out through taxes, not by fees.

- the possibility to tax only a small number of individuals with great benefits for a large number of persons (according to a social utility function) (direct redistributive effect);
- the parallelism with demand for public activity. It can be argued that in favourable growth circumstances (upswing of the business cycle), more individuals are able to pay and the demand for public goods should rise in quality, whereas in poor economic circumstances a number of person do no longer qualify as being able to pay, but also the willingness to accept certain cuts in the quality of public goods can be estimated as higher ("justice argument");
- the possibility to exempt part of the income of those well-off citizens that devote earnings to public objectives themselves (targeting argument).

2.3. Connexity principle

Proponents of the connexity principle claim that the attribution of certain tax collection from local companies and the redistribution of benefits to inhabitants would strengthen the links of responsibility and the parallelism of interest between company owners, shareholders, employees and local citizens.[6] By contributing to the benefit of the community and receiving a fair share of the benefits as well, the company would constitute special links to the local community, avoiding to focus exclusively on short time profits and rents or using the threat of relocation in times of adverse market signals (e.g. disproportionate wage rises). The core of the connexity principle would thus not be about identity or differentiation of tax rates or revenues between similar communities, but rather against a too centralized way of redistribution, which might blur the differences in structure and consequently the links of mutual responsibility. The connexity principle might thus be understood as intentionally softening one fundamental idea of taxation, that is the anonymity between taxpayers and benefit receivers.

2.4. Stability principle

The benefits paid out of the receipts from local taxes (infrastructure, energy, education, waste management etc.) have to be provided continuously, thus also in times of a business slowdown. With this in mind, the tax base for a local tax should be sufficiently stable in order to avoid pro-cyclical behaviour of tax receipts and benefits. If tax revenue fails to materialize in business slowdowns, the benefits provided by the tax financing, going both to companies and citizens

6 For example Bundesvereinigung der kommunalen Spitzenverbände (2003), chapter 1.2.

would also be reduced, thereby reducing the attractiveness to local business and resulting in a vicious circle of under-financing and worsened business prospects. In a number of cases, the normal activities of a municipality could then only be maintained via credit financing.

This scenario has already been a typical result of the continuous erosion of the tax bases (e.g., through bankruptcy of companies) and still enlarged requirements for social purposes and infrastructure purposes for certain municipalities, especially in East Germany. In the final stage, transfers from the central regional or federal government are the only measure that can reasonably step in, reducing the financial autonomy of the local authorities to zero.

To avoid such scenarios, an ideal stabilizing tax would gain sufficient revenue both in economic upturns and slowdowns. This notwithstanding, the best stabilization would lead to a more than proportional rise in revenue in upturns, which could then be used to cover deficits in downturns.

It is apparent that the fine-tuning of the tax scale, thereby finding the best degree of progression is the most important task for the authority in this regard.

The stability principle is logically opposed to the idea of sensitivity toward business cycles (see below).

2.5. Revenue principle

Closely linked to principles such as connexity and stabilization is the principle of sufficient revenue for local authorities. Although widely tested especially in the case of the Local Tax on Current Revenue and the property tax, it seems difficult to get a full theoretical picture on when a tax base can be called "sufficient". The tax scale is normally not at the focus of this debate, as it goes without saying that a certain average tax rate (for guaranteeing the revenues) can be obtained by different types of tax scales and average rates (degree of tax progression, flat rate).

Whenever it is suggested to broaden the tax base, one has to evaluate also the effects on those taxpayers which have not been eligible before (esp. enhanced property tax and enlargement to farmer or liberal professions), which would then lead to a macroeconomic analysis of additional taxes and possible supply-side behaviour. The overall redistributive effect might also be impaired. If a business tax on profits or capital which would only pose burden for the better-off is replaced by an enlarged property tax which is ultimately borne by tenants of flats, independent of their income, just dependent on the size of the flat, realistic concepts need to introduce additional redistributive measures. Unfortunately most proponents of an enlarged business tax leave out a detailed examination of this problem[7] It might therefore be very difficult to rank certain tax concepts according to their revenue-generating powers, while acknowledging the relevance of the revenue principle as such.

2.6. Reducing incentives to flee to tax havens and/or the periphery

Tax havens occur on the local stage if larger municipalities offer services for the whole, region including the periphery, but bear the costs largely alone. Due to lower taxation in the periphery, the tax base of the centre is gradually eroded whereas the level of expected public services stays the same.
Even if a harmonised surcharge on a (progressive) income tax would avoid a tax competition with regard to the LBT, the failure to charge natural persons living outside the community would not help against a population drift, people living in the periphery but working in the centre would still not contribute personally to the financing of the public goods offered in the centre. The flight to tax havens cannot be done away with the idea that it is the same usual corrective against too high taxes and too large government intervention ("exit strategy"), because it is described as a problem where also the people of the periphery wish to benefit from the public goods "bundle" and only take advantage of a possibility to avoid financing it.

It is obvious that a full harmonisation of LBTs would fulfil the criterion. But also a formula apportionment leaving leeway to the local authorities to set tax rates and tax exceptions would work (see ch. 3)

2.7. Sensitivity towards business cycles

This criterion is diametrically opposed to the stabilization concepts but it nevertheless has certain relevance for tax collection (not tax-benefit) purposes. Given that companies might not be able to pay their normal tax burden in periods of business slowdowns, when sales, wage sums, profits go down, a tax which is not responsive to such events might ultimately overburden local companies. However, these cases should normally be marginal ones and typically occur in the presence of either rather high tax rates or flat rates and only in the absence of possibilities to reduce the taxable income via balance sheet operations. In realistic settings, the criterion should therefore not be of central importance.

7 Unconvincing in this regard, for example Broer, M. (2002), while a more balanced analysis is given in Bundesvereinigung der kommunalen Spitzenverbände (2003).

2.8. Progression Neutrality

Progression neutrality is a technical criterion stemming from the fact that a local business tax should not lead to a shift in the relative burden on taxpayers (overall redistribution) as stipulated by the central income tax.

The fact that a local authority has the right to raise a specific tax should in this view not lead to a stronger or weaker progression than that determined by the central income tax. The progression exerted by the centrally chosen tax scale should thus not be altered by local authorities.

Progression neutrality should typically be evaluated in relative terms (which tax is as good in progression neutrality as an existing tax?) and when it is undisputed that the level of re-distribution is actually to be determined by the central (national) level. Then it makes sense not to cause additional progressive re-distribution or worse still, to reverse a progression. Advocates of fiscal federalism would however argue that a municipality would have the right to increase or decrease progression because the preference of the local population for a large-scale or reduced redistribution might differ considerably. Extreme cases would probably not occur, because the citizens have the right to leave the municipality and the local authorities normally lack the possibility to retaliate.

In the end relatively small distortions vis-à-vis a central administrated tax scale can normally be tolerated, so that the criteria should only rule out local taxation methods with rather extreme properties which counteract agreed distribution norms at the central level.

Table:

Criterion	Importance from theoretical viewpoint (for moderate neo-classical position)	Specific to a "local" tax ?	Politically contentious ?
Benefit/Equivalency	Medium	No	Yes
Ability-to-pay	High	No	Yes
Connexity	Medium	Yes	Somewhat
Stability	High	No	No
Revenue	Medium	No	Somewhat
Tax havens	Medium	No	Yes
Sensitivity towards business cycles	Low	No	No
Progression Neutrality	Low	Yes	Yes

3. Concepts

3.1. Enlarged local business profit tax

With an enlarged local business profit tax[8] the taxable income would be defined much broader than for a traditional corporate or income tax. The taxable companies or persons would be independent of their legal form. Although the tax rates would be in the responsibility of the local authorities, the tax would be sufficiently sensitive towards the business cycle. As long as the tax is not only targeted towards annual profits but allows for smoothing the individual tax base over several years, the tax can show a good stabilization record. It should normally also possess a very good redistribution potential.

The idea would be that most of the tax is passed through to the price of goods and services, so that it would no longer be used for downward competition.[9] However, this assumption would require further empirical testing as the set-up of this tax does not in itself address the problem of a flight to tax havens. A certain degree of harmonisation of tax base or tax rates might thus be required. Furthermore the macroeconomic effects of an enlarged local business tax cannot be stated in advance, a case-by-case analysis of both private investment reaction and the time-path of public consumption/state demand would be needed. A positive feature of the concept is the clear distinction from capital income tax/corporate tax which would need more centralisation and where a pass-through to consumers is not intended.

3.2. Enhanced tax base

There are a number of suggestions on how to enhance the tax base. While a practical concept that would only include more persons such as free professions, farmers and house owners within the business tax is similar to an enlarged local business tax (3.1). other more far-reaching ideas strive to include not only the gains on equity, but also the interest payment on debts. Depending on how large the new tax base is it remains to be analyzed who ultimately would bear the tax burden, because price reactions and tax avoidance becomes more difficult to predict. It is furthermore necessary to counterbalance the positive effects of an enhanced tax base and probably lower tax rates (including a better stability of revenues) by the strong resistance against such a step when people learn they have to pay a certain tax for the very first time.

In particular, the inclusion of farmers and house owners seems at odds with the original idea of avoiding imbalances, given that it lumps together an

8 See for example Roloff, O. (2006).
9 See Roloff, O. (2006); p.5.

immobile tax base (ground rents) with a rather mobile tax base (business, capital). However, if an enhanced tax base would include debt interest payments[10] then a good safeguard against tax flight would be achievable.

3.3. Surcharge on corporate income tax

Although a separate surcharge on the centrally administered corporate income tax would at first view be in line with the benefit principle, it falls short of achieving several other objectives. A flat-rate surcharge would leave progression intact; however, the redistributive qualities of the corporate income tax would be reduced, if it would be combined with a larger tax base (higher percentage of population eligible).

A local supplement to a central corporate income tax would indeed further spur tax competition, leave the agglomeration centres expensive and threatened by business migration whereas the outward belts would continue to profit from rich population and lower taxes because of lower need for public services, etc. [11] Finally it would weaken the link between local tax authority and the public services provided for the business. With regard to the sensitivity towards business cycles and the stability principle, most observers would tend to see the surcharge as too sensitive and thus unstable. This disadvantage is aggravated by the risk that local authorities would constantly intervene in the surcharge rate for political reasons.

3.4. Local Current Revenue Tax

The Local Current Revenue Tax would fall explicitly on private enterprise. It would have the total current revenue as a tax base, no matter how it is distributed between creditors (interest payments), labour (wages) and shareholders or owners (profits). The local authorities would have the possibility[12] to apply a municipal percentage to a basic harmonised rate.

The Local Current Revenue Tax would serve the "ability to pay"-principle in the best fashion. As it is also taking into account business cycles, thereby

10 See for example Jarass, L. (2006), p.13.

11 Therefore sceptical to the SVR-suggestions among many others Junkernheinrich, M. (2005): Landkreistag Nordrhein-Westfalen, Eildienst 7/8-2005 as well as Jarass, L. (2006). Critical points (enforced tax competition, larger gap between rich and poor municipalities) are also referred by Friedrich, E. (o.J.).

12 This right to apply a municipal percentage to a harmonised tax rate would entail no difference to the current system in Germany.

avoiding aggravating negative situations for the private sector,[13] it scores well with regard to the connexity principle.

The idea would be to put a fair burden on business[14] for financing its infrastructure needs. In general even though wages and interest payments are part of the tax base, the LCR Tax should possess a good redistributive capacity and at least an average sensitivity to business cycles.[15] Elements of a LCR Tax have been used and advocated before, however the argument to tax interest payment on debt capital was always challenged and recent reforms ran into problems of including small businesses whose exemption had been deemed necessary in order to maintain an attractive shopping environment in urban areas.

The disadvantages of this tax can be seen in that it disfavours companies with seasonal cycles in revenues, it is disadvantageous also for companies with a high share of part-time employment. Some of the arguments that are normally used against a wage bill tax apply as well as the LCR Tax would contain a wage bill component.

3.5. Formula Apportionment of a central business tax

Formula apportionment means that the tax base of a business tax is distributed via a centrally agreed formula. The residence of the company would not be the only criterion to determine which local entity has the right to tax. Formula apportionment exists for corporate taxes on the national level in the US, Canada and Switzerland and has been suggested for the corporate taxes and capital gains taxes in the economic literature.[16] With regard to *local* business taxes it has not

---

13 To replace the so-called council tax based on property by a "Local Income Tax" was a major campaign argument of the LDP in the UK elections 2005. The Local Current Revenue Tax would however only fall on private enterprise and would thus have even better redistributive characteristics.

14 The discrimination against business income vis-à-vis other types of income is economically justified because it can hardly be argued that private citizens - even with the same aggregate income - would use infrastructure in *the same way* that businesses do (airports, road traffic, extra lanes, congestion, exclusion of vast territory from the public sphere). The existence of business reshapes cities and regions. Furthermore businesses form a legal entity of its own and are simply more than an aggregate of its owners or shareholders.

15 Müller, A. (2004); Friedrich, E. (o.J.).; Scherf, W. (2002): Die anrechenbare Wertschöpfungssteuer - Ein Vorschlag zur Gewerbesteuerreform, in: Spiegel der Forschung 1/2002 (19. Jg.); p. 70-74.

16 The 2001 report by the European Commission suggested formula apportionment for corporate taxes as an alternative in the Internal Market. See, Fuest, C. et al. (2006), p.2.

been at the centre of the debate; however the principal situation is similar as the tax base consists of business profits.

By applying formula apportionment to a corporate tax (between regions, federal states or EU Member States) or to a local business tax (between municipalities), the notion of autonomy of the jurisdiction is of course diminished. The loss of local links and of local autonomy in determining the tax exemptions might thus be felt as a disadvantage by local decision makers. As the formula apportionment should guarantee a local tax basis within appropriate limits, the incentive to work as efficiently as possible with the tax receipts, for example to support business-related infrastructure or education and training facilities, might be reduced. On the other hand, the formula apportionment is best apt to avoid the erosion of a tax base. The incentives to make monetary gains just by changing the place of residence or production will be diminished, so that location decisions will be productivity-led and ultimately growth-oriented. A tax base apportioned via a formula will stay sufficiently broad and there will be no race to the bottom in tax rates. A further good feature of formula apportionment is that a prior harmonisation of the tax base is not strictly necessary.[17] It is sufficient to announce the percentage of the tax base to which a certain local entity has taxation rights, while leaving it largely to the lower level on how to calculate the tax base. Welfare-reducing effects of formula apportionment seem to relate to rather theoretical, not very robust cases;[18] the attractiveness of profit shifting by multinational firms is reduced as well as the idea to work with various tax exemptions to counteract the effect of a higher average tax rate.[19] Certainly, the usefulness of formula apportionment depends on the type of formula used. In this regard, capital and labour (wage sum) combined or the cash-flow would lead to less distortions than relying

17 On the pros and cons of formula apportionment of a company tax in a review of recent studies see Eggert, W.; Haufler, A. (2006): Company tax coordination cum tax rate competition; Discussion Paper 2006--11; Department of Economics; University of Munich; see especially on the formula apportionment without harmonised tax base, p.15-16. Fuest, C. et al. (2006) take as their basis a full harmonisation of the tax base as proposed in the Commission study of 2001. Not surprisingly the overall tax basis shrinks partly because of loss-offset, but theoretically also because part of the profits of EU multinationals would then no longer be taxable by EU jurisdictions. Within the EU, some smaller countries that would usually attract book profits would lose, while larger countries with a higher share of employment, sales or property would relatively gain. The important point is however, that formula apportionment can work without harmonisation of the tax base, so that smaller countries would have an incentive to recalculate.

18 Ibid; p.1-2.

19 The majority of empirical studies supports the idea that both profit shifting and investment decisions are guided by average and not marginal tax rates; ibid; p.7-8.

exclusively on capital or labour.[20] Also other weights like sales, macroeconomic or industry figures might work in practice and in combination.[21] The weighting according to sales, macroeconomic or industry figures might - at worst - lead to "too high" taxes, but not to tax erosion, the problem to which a solution had been sought. When transferring these general arguments to local taxes, the question of internalising fiscal externalities enforces the support for an agreed central formula apportionment, maintaining local autonomy in the tax rates.[22] In any case, formula apportionment mostly improves the situation when compared to no coordination at all. To conclude, when rated in terms of best protection against detrimental tax rate competition and tax evasion the formula apportionment solution should thus be ranked highly. Furthermore, formula apportionment shows a good sensitivity towards business cycles and a very good redistributive capacity.

4. Conclusion

Efficient redistribution lies at the heart of an optimal tax system. If the problem would only be how to finance public goods, fees, custom duties or maybe profits from some state-owned enterprises would also do the job. However, we have argued that redistribution capabilities of an efficient market system are vital for the acceptance of market forces, competition and the need to adapt individually. This redistribution has then to be carried out as efficient as possible. Here it seems to be clear that tax rates and tax bases do not have to be harmonised across the board, because the preferences of people in different jurisdictions will probably differ. But accepting this variety also means that local and regional authorities need measures to protect their efficient tax system against erosion of

---

20 It is obvious that if neither the tax rate nor the tax base is harmonised, the weighting (apportionment formula) has to be agreed upon by consensus and thus be harmonised in order to safeguard the objectives of formula apportionment as such (ibid, p. 17, in this regard, the actual system in the US is suboptimal.). Given that autonomy on setting the tax rate is politically intended (no total harmonisation), the real choice is thus only between formula apportionment with a harmonised tax base and formula apportionment without a harmonised tax base, which can both work under realistic assumptions. Eggert and Haufler however see formula apportionment rather as a second-best solution if tax rate harmonisation is not achievable (p.20). Similarly, Sterdyniak, H. (2005) is sceptical to the Commission's idea of formula apportionment and considers a discussion on harmonised minimum rates as unavoidable (p.28-29).

21 Cp. Eggert/Haufler (2006) p.17.

22 For local taxes Runkel, M.; Schjelderup, G. (2007): The Choice of apportionment factors under formula apportionment, CES-ifo Working Paper No. 2072, Public Finance August 2007; p. 3. show that welfare effects of a centrally agreed formula are positive because a centrally agreed formula internalises fiscal externalities, furthermore the optimal apportionment factors would include capital and not only labor.

tax base and an adaptation of the level of redistribution (and other public goods) that is provoked from "outside". If these measures cannot be administered unilaterally, intervention from a higher level is justified. Some basic principles can be agreed at central level and still a sufficient degree of autonomy can be maintained (e.g. in the model of formula apportionment like in the US). New challenges - especially in an enlarged EU - however might need new replies.

In this context, the Local Current Revenue tax is sometimes excluded from the possibilities to design an improved tax for local authorities. But this seems to be due to the immediate fear of losing the tax base, be that on a national or even on an international scale (usual globalization argument). However one has to ask whether this is not foremost an issue of creating an optimal international regime for investment and capital flows, and not as an inherent weakness of a local current revenue tax. On top of this, when discussing the pros and cons of types of taxes, certain voices do not necessarily search for a solid financing of local public goods (including redistribution), but eo ipso for additional relief for private business or worse even, for spurring a political debate on the "fair share for the state." This is then carried out by fostering the idea of enlarging the number of people eligible to pay instead of broadening the tax base in monetary terms or increasing the reliability of sufficient tax receipts.

It comes as no surprise that the tasks of local communities stay the same or even aggravate in financial needs in times of economic slowdowns (esp. social assistance). In view of the fact that a solution for solid financing is a most pressing problem, the rejection of a Current Revenue Tax seems to be premature.[23] Although its is a worthwhile task to examine who will bear the costs of a tax and what price and production effects might occur, one should not forget the redistributive function and objectives of any tax system. If more growth results from a broader spread of income (be that income for the state or non-market income of citizens) not the least via a better balance between consumption and investment, the "raison d'être" of a redistributive tax system is already fulfilled.

---

23 The German Council of Economic Experts (SVR) (2001/02); Ciphers 380-386, rejected the Current Revenue Tax on grounds of its absolute effect on internationally mobile capital and because it falls also on labour. It seems however difficult to a imagine a tax raised at the business level that has not any absolute effect on any factor (capital, labour). Moreover, with regard to the minimizing of distortions between the factors the CRT scores quite well.

Literature

Bundesvereinigung der kommunalen Spitzenverbände (Federal Association of Municipal Central Organisations) (2003): Vorschlag für eine modernisierte Gewerbesteuer; Cologne

Eggert, W.; Haufler, A. (2006): Company tax coordination cum tax rate competition; Discussion Paper 2006--11; Department of Economics; University of Munich

Friedrich, E. (o.J.): Reformmodelle, www.kommunaler-wettbewerb.de

Fuest, C.; Hemmelgarn, T.; Ramb, F. (2006): How would formula apportionment in the EU affect the distribution and the size of the corporate tax base? An analysis based on German multinationals; Deutsche Bundesbank, Dp series "Economic Studies" 20/2006

Jarass, L. (2006): Grundsätzliche und aktuelle Fragen der Steuer- und Finanzpolitik; (revised version of a speech on 24.10.2005); Deutsche Hochschule für Verwaltungswissenschaften, Speyer

Junkernheinrich, M. (2005): Landkreistag Nordrhein-Westfalen, Eildienst 7/8-2005

Linscheidt, B.; Truger, A. (1997): Reform des Kommunalsteuersystems; in: Vierteljahreshefte zur Wirtschaftsforschung 3/4-1997; S. 382-394

Müller, A. (2004): Die Reformlüge, Munich

Mundorf, H. (2006) : Nachhilfe für den Steuermann, Recension of: Tipke, K. in: Handelsblatt, 9 June 2006

Musgrave, R. (1959): The Theory of Public Finance. A Study in Public Economy Theory; New York

Roloff, O. (2006): Reform der Unternehmensteuer im fiskalischen Wettbewerb, in: CWG-Dialog 1/2006; p. 4-6

Runkel, M.; Schjelderup, G. (2007): The Choice of apportionment factors under formula apportionment, CES-ifo Working Paper No. 2072, Public Finance August 2007

Scherf, W. (2002): Die anrechenbare Wertschöpfungssteuer - Ein Vorschlag zur Gewerbesteuerreform, in: Spiegel der Forschung 1/2002 (19. Jg.); p. 70-74.

Sterdyniak, H. (2005): Taxation in Europe, towards more competition or more co-ordination, OFCE Working Paper, No.2005-19

SVR (Sachverständigenrat; German Council of Economic Experts)(2001/02): Jahresgutachten 2001/2002. (http://www.sachverstaendigenrat-wirtschaft.de/download/gutachten/01_ges.pdf); Ciphers 380-386

Tipke, K. (2006): Ein Ende dem Einkommensteuerwirrwarr?; Cologne

Kolibri 360 GmbH
Ferdinand-Jühlke-Straße 7
99095 Erfurt, Deutschland
produktsicherheit@kolibri360.de

Druck:
CPI Druckdienstleistungen GmbH
im Auftrag der
Kolibri 360 GmbH
Ferdinand-Jühlke-Str. 7
99095 Erfurt